quantified as good or bad. Instead I'm starting to see it as a process engaged in by almost everybody, on a daily basis.

Let me try to explain —
When people arrive in the office in the morning, it is clear they have chosen the accessories that go with their outfits. Even when done badly, the process involves design choices. If you order a car and decide which features it should come with, you are making design decisions. Where you decide to tidy up your bookshelves and come up with a classification system based on heights of books (girls) or alphabetically (boys) or even by colour of spine (me), that is also a design decision. Likewise, if you are lucky enough to have a garden, then the choice of plants, the pots they go in and the configuration and spacing of the vegetable rows are all, in my view, design decisions. The only value judgement I would care to make is whether things have improved or deteriorated through the implementation of these decisions. Right, so that's sorted out.

Design is the activity of improving things by rearranging them in a way that will improve them. This can be an improvement in the look, feel or functioning, or an enhancement of the manufacturing process or delivery of the aforementioned object. The important thing to remember is that it is something that can be done by everyone. Therefore anyone can improve their own or others' lives through the application of design.

Having defined this means that I can now get on and show you what interests me in design at the moment. Just like a chaos theorist, I believe that a pattern will emerge from all the stuff we are currently being bombarded with. However, it's such a chaotic and hyperactive field right now, with so many contradictory opinions, ideas and influences, that I have been forced to classify the material into bite-sized pieces more commonly referred to as chapters, in an attempt to bring some order to the interior world of Tom Dixon. To do this, I have found it convenient to use some of the *isms* usually applied to art or architecture to define periods or styles. These at least will allow me to define in a crude way some of the thoughts – so here goes.

TOM DIXON
INTERIOR
WORLDS

RIZZOLI
NEW YORK

Contents

First published in the United States of America in 2009 by
Rizzoli International Publications, Inc.
300 Park Avenue South
New York, NY 10010
www.rizzoliusa.com

Originally published in the United Kingdom in 2008 by
Conran Octopus Limited,
a part of Octopus Publishing Group,
2–4 Heron Quays
London E14 4JP
www.octopusbooks.co.uk

2009 2010 2011 2012 / 10 9 8 7 6 5 4 3 2 1

ISBN: 978-0-8478-3239-2

Library of Congress Control Number: 2008934814

Printed in China

RHINOCEROS

1 — Materialism

I don't know about you, but for me it all started very early, somewhere between the sandpit and the modelling clay. I was always a mucky little boy and some of my earliest memories involve being told not to play with my food, which I still remember as being a *major* injustice. What a shame not to play with food, I thought, aged four, when the possibility of creating mountains out of mashed potato or portraits out of toast seemed a better use of these raw materials than simply consuming them.

It was later still, in pottery class, that more practical examples revealed the hidden potential of substances. Formless, cold, greasy clay was transformed into towering, thin-walled vessels at the potter's wheel and then, as if by magic, fired at a very high temperature in an oven to become stone. What an inspiration, I thought, to have the promises hidden within even the murkiest lumps of mud revealed in such an amazing way.

Much, much later (I was a late developer), I was taught to use an oxyacetylene welding torch, and through darkened goggles a whole new world was defined for me. Gazing at the pool of molten metal as I fused two bits of steel together, I became aware that, with a small amount of knowledge, fire and some metal, I could make almost anything I dreamed up. How fabulous and liberating to discover a material that was malleable and ductile, that could be attached in so many ways, through soldering or riveting, folding or fusing, with flames and with hammers. Here was a material that could be as shiny as a mirror or as rough as rock. Something, even, that could start the day as a rusty piece of scrap metal and, through manipulation and application of a $1000°C$ flame, become a comforting wedge of banknotes in my pocket by the evening (thanks to my early appreciation of commerce).

Testing the limits —
It didn't feel anything other than normal to test out the limits and possibilities of this extraordinary series of materials. In fact, somehow it almost felt like an in-built genetic predisposition. Humankind, blessed with an inquisitive nature, must have begun very early to be intrigued by the potential of converting materials into structures for shelter, into artefacts for increasing productivity, into tools for the processing of food, and later into status symbols or objects of devotion. This must have started with sticks and twigs, as evidenced by the primitive tools used by chimpanzees and gorillas, and then progressed at one point to the bones and hides of animals. The possibilities inherent in stone for making hammers, knives or cooking implements are where the skill and accumulated knowledge of man began to show. His skill in organizing and processing material into constructions and artefacts at first made his life easier and later became part of systems of organization and of status.

In that respect, nothing much has changed today. Whether the design is of an object or an interior or a vehicle, materials are always going to be the basic building blocks and the departure point for all that follows. Accordingly, a fascination for materials and all that can be done with them has to be a prerequisite for any designer.

For a designer living in the modern world, this understanding of the possibilities inherent in materials has unlimited scope. The available palette is almost enough to make us collapse with visual and sensory overload. Just look at the extraordinary promise and choice – the rough and the smooth, the synthetic and the natural (or a synthesis of the two), the transparent, the fluorescent and the glowing, the heavy and the ultra-light, the reflective and the light-absorbent, the water-repellent and the adhesive. What's more, acoustic ceramics, flexible glass, inflatable steel, super-gels and soluble plastics are but a few of the new materials that contradict the preconceived nature of their physical qualities.

Despite the amazing array of possibilities, the contemporary world is filled with materials that masquerade as one another. Plastics, being of any shape, density, colour or texture, have been guilty of passing themselves off as versions of leather, wood, metal and glass. With the advancing virtuosity of printing methods, anything is now possible, from a telephone in faux marble to a carpet in pine-floorboard effect. For a while, particularly in the 1970s, an ironic take on these possibilities was popular but, as with fashion, the progression is cyclic. The more I think about all these design books, design museums and design whatevers, the more I realize that what is celebrated or dismissed as good or bad design is going to be superseded within a decade or so anyway. A lot of what is classed as good design is actually just good fashion for the moment. Faking a surface is something postmodern times were very anxious to demonstrate, but then inevitably discarded when the approach become more serious again.

The difference now is that the quality of processes has so improved that there is often no clear division between natural materials and synthetics. The term 'natural' is pushed to the extreme as some synthetics contain natural ingredients, further testing definitive classification. Fakes are getting so good that people are becoming indifferent to the once-perceived cheapness of imitation. Reconstituted leathers are now indistinguishable from the real thing, and more recently the lower end companies such as Ikea have blurred the distinction between real and fake even more.

In addition, it may well become acceptable to specify fake fur, ebony-effect dashboards or mock-croc upholstery as the authentic sources of these fabulous substances and textures rapidly decline. No longer is it politically correct to sport a zebra-skin rug, elephant-foot umbrella stand or ebony chess set. Now that more and more materials such as plastic are formless or can take any shape or any texture, the big challenge for the designer is how to define that material in its own right rather than faking a natural finish of some sort – what do you do to make it seem appealing?

Opening the floodgates —
As we are only at the dawn of our exploration into materials (the invention of plastic was not much more than a hundred years ago), the answers are there for the taking. The revolution happening in technology means that we are being liberated from the historic constraints of conventional materials or surfaces. The ability to change a material in form, chemical composition and physical property is unbounded and without preconception. Through digital printing and rapid prototyping we are now capable of making just about anything out of anything, opening the floodgates to unlimited variations in pattern, shape and texture.

And that is just the beginning! Soon there will be a new generation of completely unforeseen materials made from modified genetic matter, grown or manufactured by microbes and nanorobots, and capable of being processed into extraordinary objects. This is a form of liberation for the product designer, who has previously been constrained by the limitations of existing machines and tooling that give objects a series of predisposed shapes. Soon, anything that can be imagined will be able to be made.

This presents us with an exciting future, but also with the horrific possibility of being deluged with unstoppable waves of hideous, malformed or unnecessary stuff made just because we can! Think of the tidal wave of poor-quality two-dimensional materials that has engulfed us since the advent of digital printing and easy-to-use graphic software. Everyone is now a graphic designer, with neither constraints nor training. Try to imagine what that could look like in three dimensions – you can start to understand the potential downside.

Already we are seeing this prospect realized. As the typical designer gets more and more involved with the virtual environment on screen, the less they think about raw materials and how they can be worked. Designers are increasingly unaware of what a material can do and how it behaves in certain circumstances.

Eventually, though, everything will be grown in baths of hi-tech gunk, replicating what's on screen, and any development going on in your brain will be made three-dimensionalized and materialized by machines. This complete break with the past will unleash any amount of creativity, spawning objects that have scarcely even been dreamed of and, of course, an accompanying horror show of inappropriate and superfluous product.

Material world —
Nevertheless, there is a limit to people's desire to surround themselves with an artificial environment, and the general enthusiasm of the 1960s to envelop oneself in synthetic materials seems to have vanished. No longer are we keen to dress from head to toe in Bri-Nylon, polyester and Lurex. Gone are the all-over patterned Formica kitchens, vinyl wipe-clean wallpapers and giant PVC bean-bags. Advertising campaigns for homeware companies are currently much more likely to stress the solid, honest qualities and natural provenance of their products. The advertisers recognize their customers' emotional attachment to

nature that cannot be removed from their DNA. Of course, there is always a hunger for the artificial or novel, for increased performance through scientifically improved man-made materials, and for applications that are technologically driven, such as telephones, microwave ovens, televisions and cars. But when it comes to living and recreation, nature seems to have regained the advantage over synthetics.

Far from viewing this as a regression, however, I can see only opportunity and potential in an updated way of using of natural substances in contemporary design. Rather than rejecting traditional materials as old-fashioned and no longer relevant in a modern age, innovative designers find themselves suddenly able to harness new methods of processing, manipulating, cutting, gluing and fabricating existing materials in ways that would have previously been impossible.

My recent experiences in this field have been with bamboo. Traditionally used for woven furniture and cooking implements, this is also a superlative building material, its superior strength/weight ratio, attractive appearance, low cost and extraordinarily fast growth characteristics making it potentially one of the most important readily available materials of the future. This is because of the current availability of new processing machinery and bonding agents that allow us to treat what was previously a 'craft' material as a contemporary resource for modern industry. As the bamboo poles can be machined into slats that are then compressed into blocks, it can be treated as a modern engineering material.

During my working life, there have been few advances in materials or processes that have touched the furniture or product world. How frustrating not to work in a time such as the early 1960s, when wartime developments in technology and materials science suddenly became available and affordable. Releasing the potential for new shapes, new functions, new colours and transparencies, they liberated the designer and allowed the possibility of creating things that had never before existed. But things are now changing rapidly, and suddenly a whole new landscape of materials and processing is developing. We are living at a time when new materials and significantly different ways of making things are being developed that will have a massive and unforeseen impact.

This new frontier is being opened up by such processes as nanotechnology, biochemistry and genetic engineering, leading to a future that could be a golden age for designers, allowing them to play God. Imagine growing a family of sofas and chairs like a herd of cows, all to custom sizes, with no seams and with in-built foam. Reflect on the possibility of growing whole buildings using enhanced coral deposition, providing an extra habitat for marine life as we build underwater, just as nature intended. The last example is not a fantastical vision of the distant future, but a prototype developed by the architect and marine scientist Wolf H. Hilbertz. Involving electrodeposition of minerals in sea

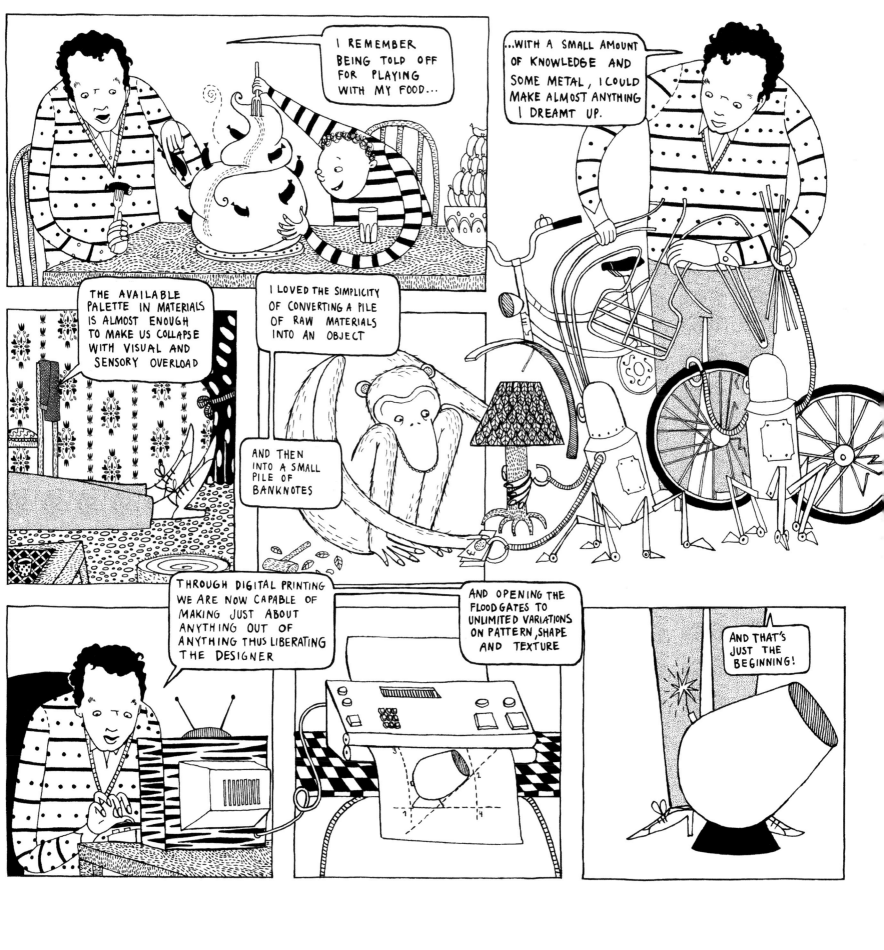

water, the process employs low-voltage DC currents to deposit calcium- and magnesium-rich substrates on a metallic mesh as a base for the recreation of coral. It is aimed not just at regeneration, but also at the building of underwater cities, yet it is really quite low-tech and achievable.

A genuinely new age —
The potential for defining how something grows empowers the designer, turning them into somebody who can suddenly do more. That is going to be the beautiful thing about the future – you will be able to make new things and new shapes because materials will behave differently. We're living in a completely new stage in the development of materials, I think, I hope, I believe.

The ages of man are described in terms of materials, from the Stone Age through the Bronze Age to the Iron Age, each referring to materials as a reason for progress. Since then we have passed through other ages, including what could be called the Industrial Age, the Steam Age and the Plastic Age. Now into a new century and a new millennium, we have added many new and composite materials to our palette, and the advancements are appearing so rapidly that they are overlapping. We find ourselves in a combination of ages – the Space Age, the Nuclear Age, the Cybernetic Age. What ages are yet to be added?

All too often designers will start with the object's shape, its function or a brief. I've always felt an urge to try to start as far back as a project will allow me. In the most extreme scenario that may even mean starting with the extraction of the raw materials, like these Cornish tin miners of the 1930s.

The way a material is processed always has an impact on the intrinsic properties of that material, and potentially on the cost of the final product. Increasingly, though, we will find that its effect on the environment and its impact on the workforce will also be factors that are taken into account. The deforestation of the Amazon rainforest in Brazil is one such issue.

Wood going into the factory at a
furniture manufacturer in Lithuania.

Above and right — The bark is peeled from logs,
which can then be sliced or sawn to form veneer.

Hot slag from a Russian nickel foundry in Norilsk, western Siberia, glows as it is poured into a slag pit at dusk.

A worker is silhouetted by red-hot metal at the copper foundry in Norilsk, western Siberia.

Glass being heated before being blown
by Peter Layton, a glass-maker based in
London, England.

Dry-stone walling specialist Dave Hannaford
at work on Dartmoor, in Devon, England.

Worker welding while wearing a makeshift protective visor.

A labourer makes earthenware lamps at a workshop in India.

Smoothing wet concrete.

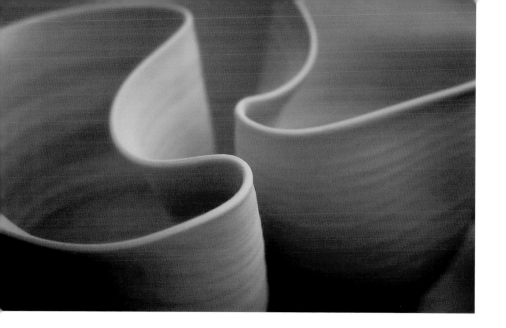

Artists decorate large pieces of pottery in Jingdezhen, in Jiangxi province, China. The city has a 1,700-year history of china production.

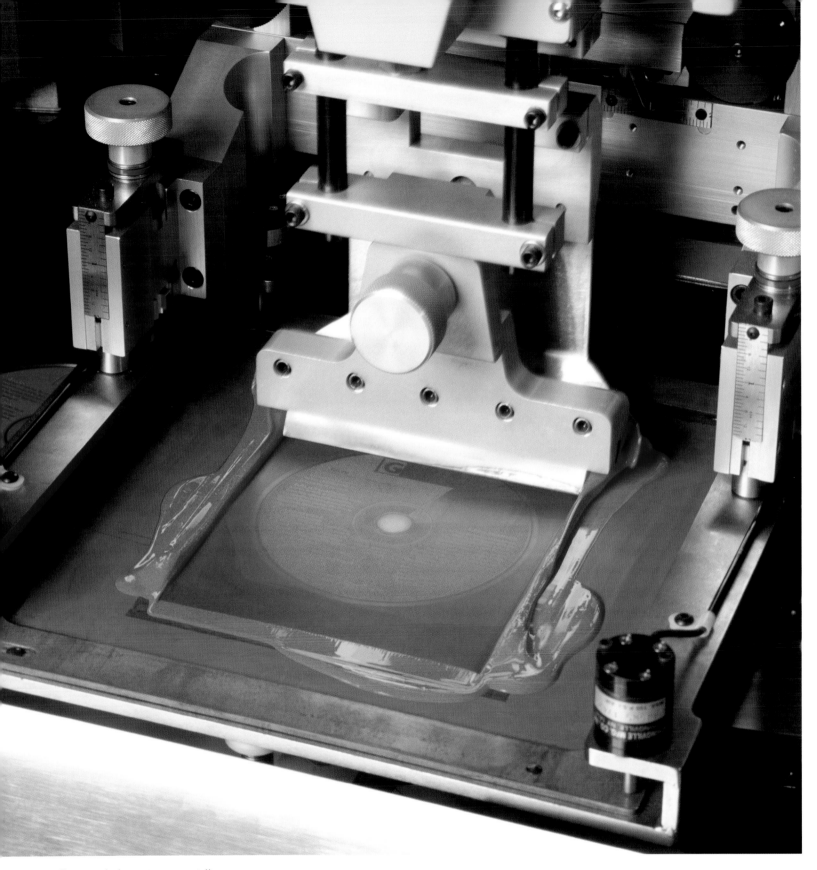

Screen printing onto compact discs.

A high-tech textile mill.

A bobbin lacemaker at work. How materials perform when manipulated and formed through a variety of techniques will always underpin a designer's work.

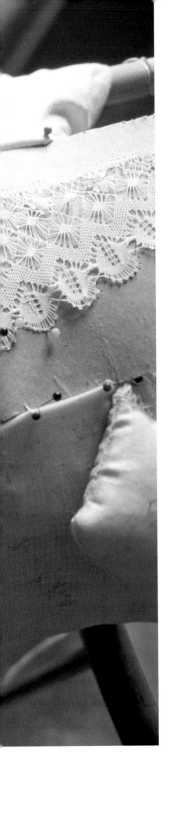

Even the waste pile offers clues to a potential for increased efficiency in production, and also ready-made shapes that could be exploited for another object. I never leave a scrap bin unexplored.

Right — Aluminium scrap collected for recycling.

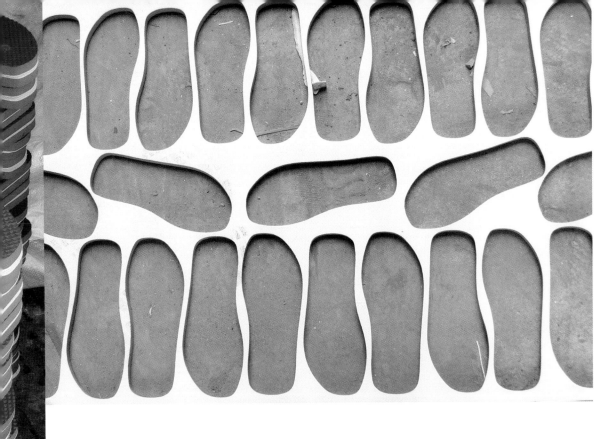

Flip-flop sandals and their waste in production.
Scrap metal, paper, plastic and waste for recycling.
Cans that have been recycled as a sort of chain mail.

Pages 34 – 37 — The look and feel of objects at the
end of their lives is all too often ignored.

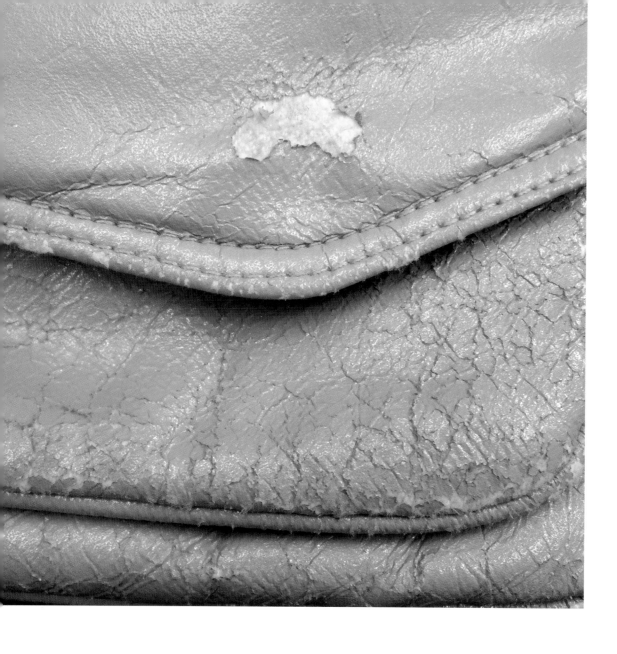

Above — Decaying polystyrene.

Right — A crumbling brick wall.

Pages 38 – 43 — The obsession with the shiny, the blinging and the brand-new may be fading, but an intrinsic knowledge of how materials deteriorate and decay in use is essential even at the very earliest stages of designing objects.

Pages 44 – 55 — The stacks of stuff in the hardware store, in the
builder's yard or on the factory floor speak of endless possibilities
in shape, texture and construction.

Pellets made from the material used to manufacture artificial heart valves are melted down to find a new life as plastic wine corks.

Aluminium ingots in a foundry awaiting smelting.

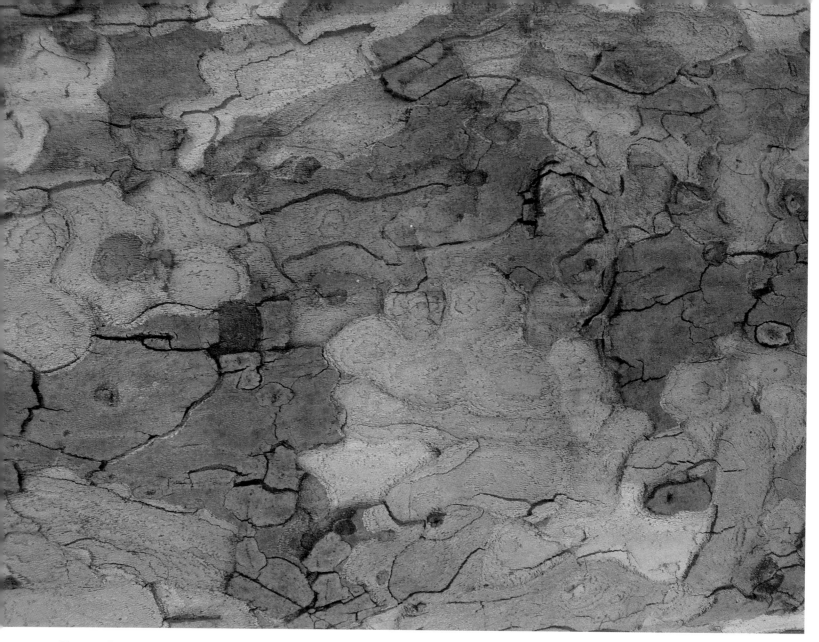

The growth patterns and weathering characteristics of natural materials
should always be considered in their application.

58 — 59 Materialism

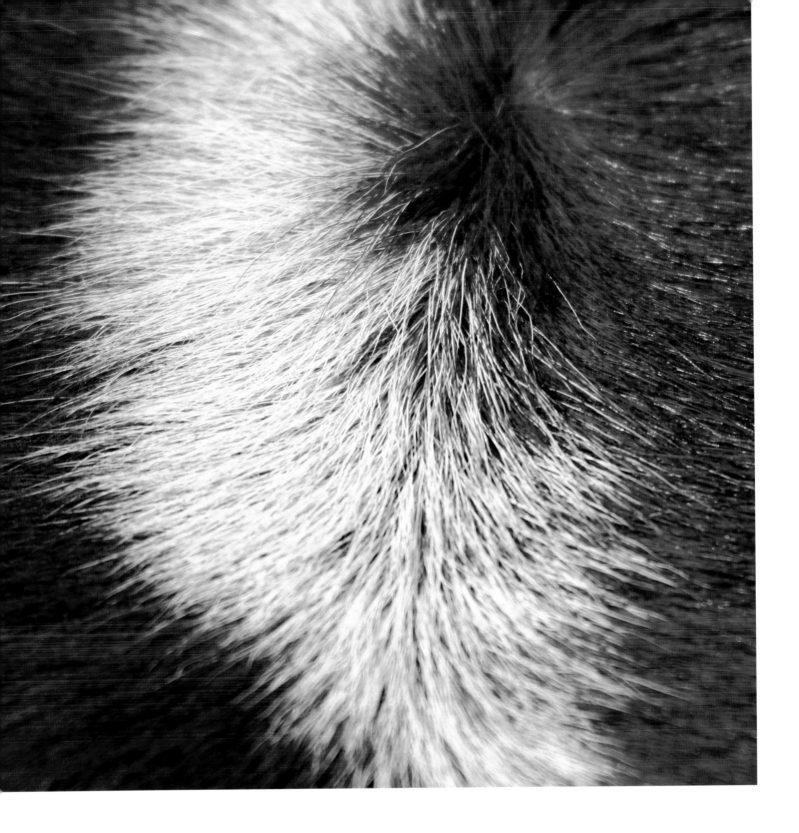

Left — Horsehair.

Above — Crocodile skin.

Pages 60 – 67 — Nature's infinite variations of texture and colour
are an extraordinary lesson in the unlimited potential of materials
to suit different situations, whether structural, functional, defensive,
protective or decorative.

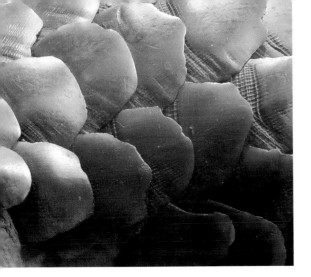

Above — Armadillo shell.

Right — Inner crystalized fossil.

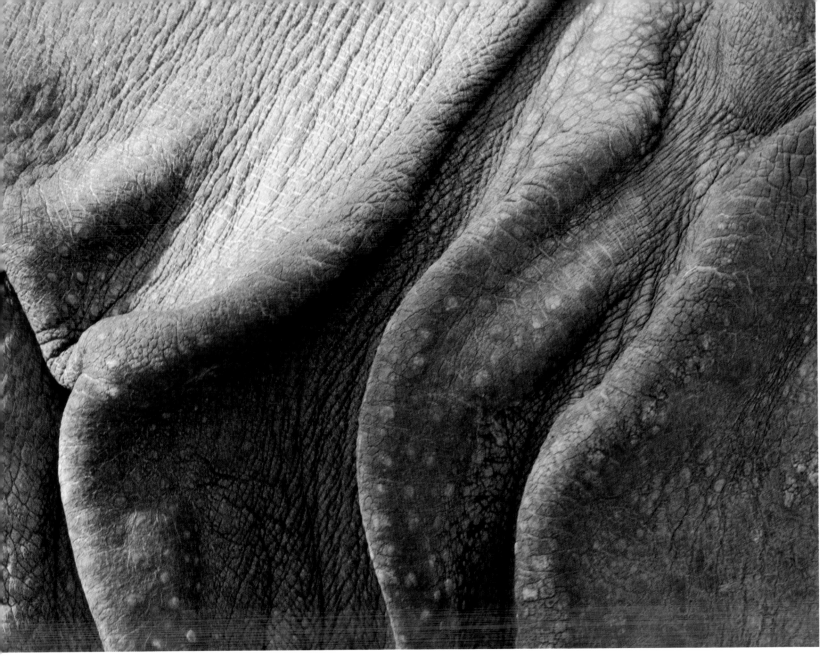

Above — Rhinoceros hide.

Right — A pufferfish.

Fish scales and their patterns.

The Slovakian-born designer Tomas Gabzdil Libertiny, who is based in the
Netherlands, devised a unique collaboration with nature. In 2006 he created a series
of wax vases by allowing a colony of bees to construct their honeycomb around
a vase-shaped space in a beehive. Each vase took 40,000 bees a week to make.
Appropriately, these flower vases are made from a material that is a by-product
of the nectar of flowers. It is also a great example of how the economical and
creative use of materials has long been explored by species other than humans.

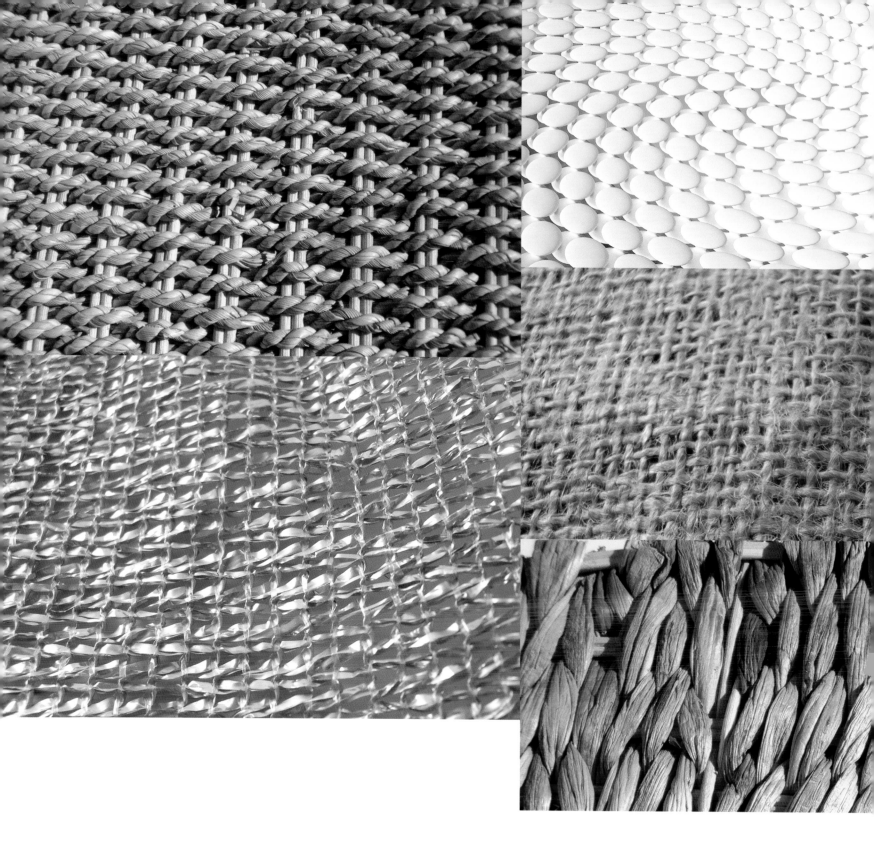

The weaving, knitting or other linking of linear material to process into textiles, mesh, baskets, fences or clothing is one of the earliest manufacturing skills, and the techniques are still valid today.

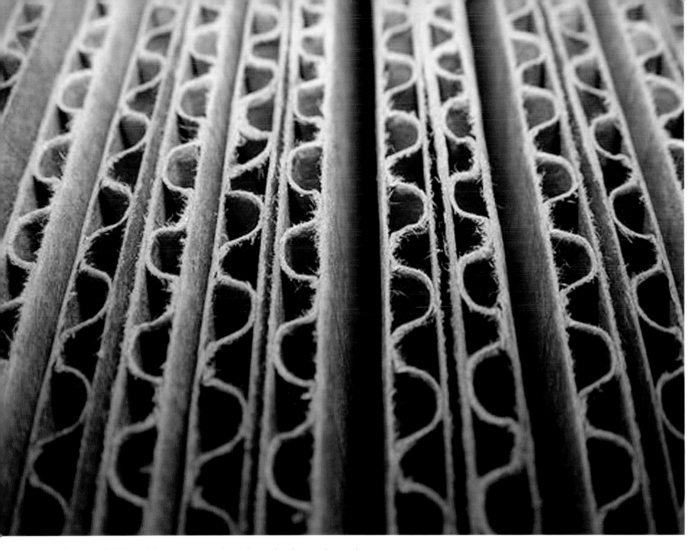

Above and right — These constructions show the decorative and structural potential of cellular, triangulated, corrugated and foamed constructions from industry, science and nature.

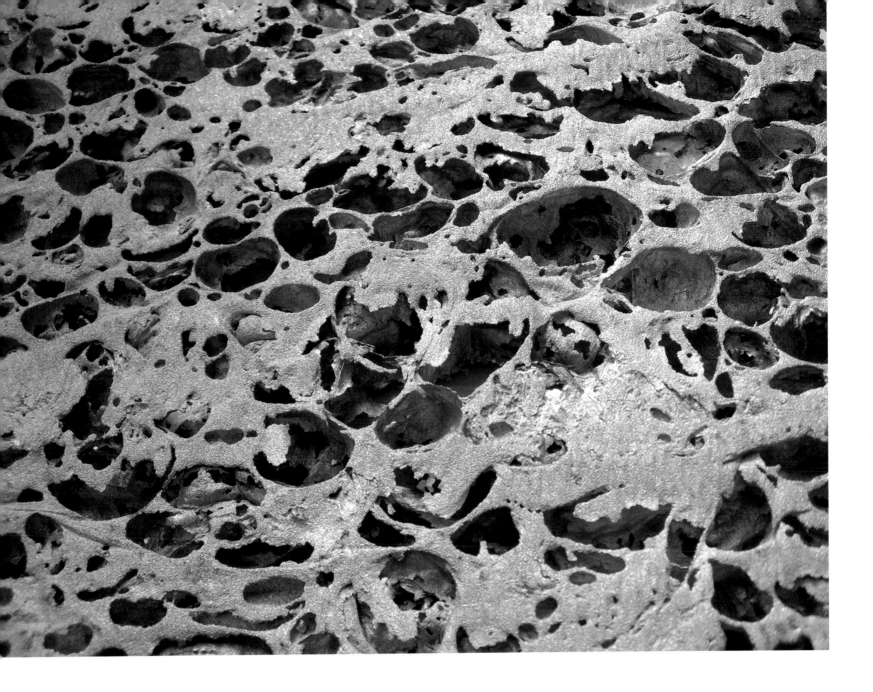

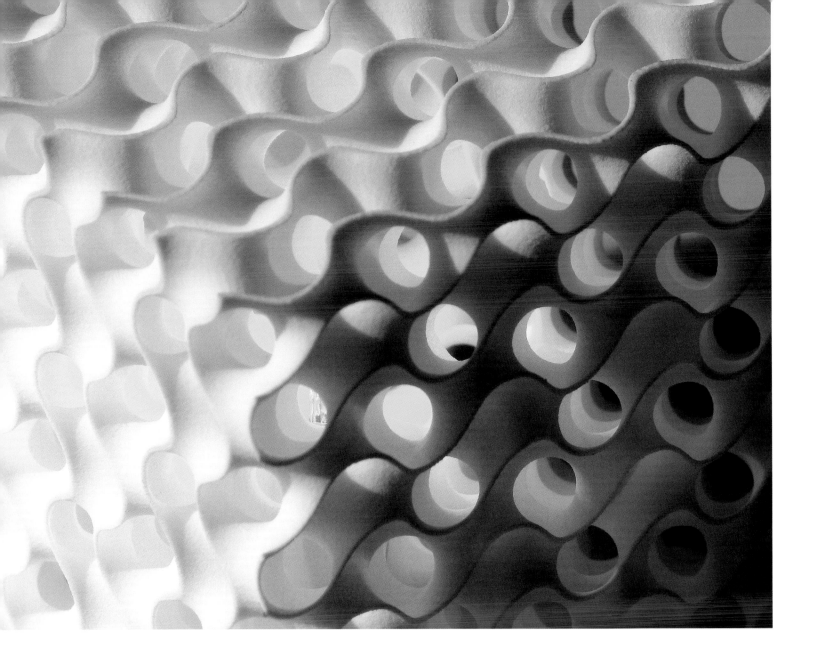

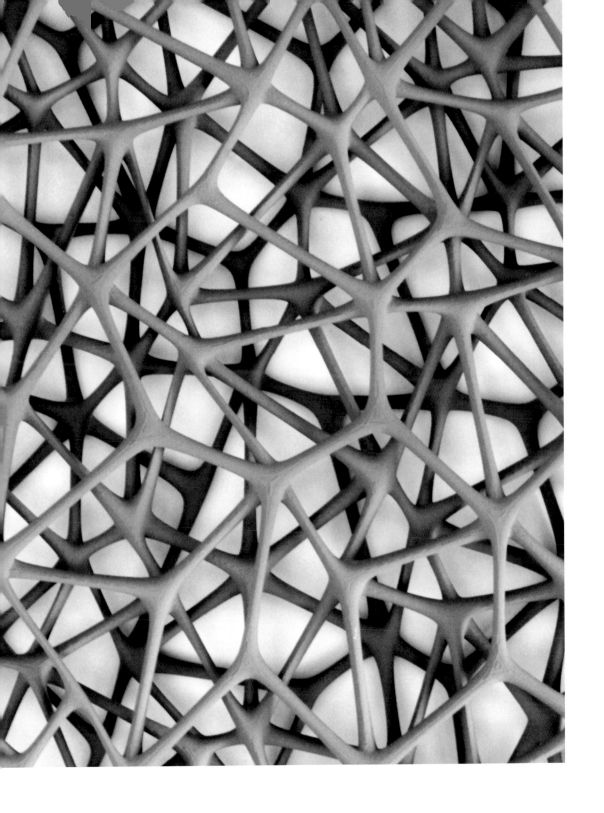

Above — 'Petit Jardin', a garden bench by Dutch-born London-based designer
Tord Boontje, featuring laser-cut graphic forms in powder-coated steel.

Right — Hand-blown glass ice basket by London-based designer Peter Layton.

Pages 80 – 88 — Modern man-made materials such as glass, metal and plastic
do not always come with intrinsic form, texture or colour, which poses extra
challenges to the designer. What is the natural state of such materials?

Left — Monoblock rapid prototyping chair by Patrick Jonin.

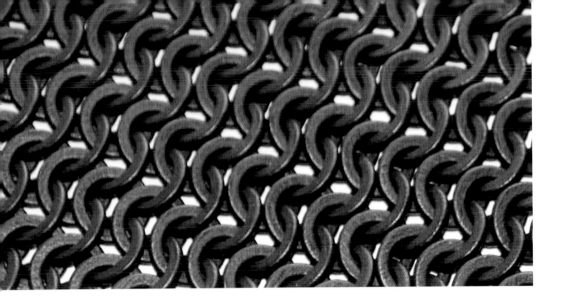

92 — 93 Materialism

The micro factory —

It was a factory visit (as usual) that started me thinking about plastics. I had gone to select some colours for a new chair, and as I was walking past the industrial machines I noticed a sad, misshapen blob of multicoloured plastic on the floor. It was a bit like the joke-shop dog poo that amused me so much as a kid, but delicately coloured in multiple shades of red, pink, white, baby blue and dark indigo. This lump of material had a charm all of its own. as most plastic production is monocoloured and in precise, crisp, engineered shapes, owing to the constraints of the moulding process. It turned out to be called a 'purge', which is both the process of emptying the bowels of an extrusion machine when changing colours and the by-product of that purpose.

I took it home, using it as a doorstop and paperweight, and then an idea struck me. The problem any self-propelled designer has, if they want to enter the complex and hi-tech world of plastics, is the tooling. First there is the extortionate cost of it and then, once the tool had been invested in, the inflexibility of the production process (requiring, for example, minimum colour baths – usually at least one ton – and large production batches). If I were able to run my extrusion machine in purge mode the whole time, I could form the plastic while it was still hot and then form objects in any colour I chose, pulling and pushing it in a process closer to pastry-making than plastic production. Colours could be changed at will, and objects large and small could be made on a whim.

A small extrusion machine was modified to make a tagliatelle-sized ribbon of plastic and, with a bit of adjustment to the machine running speed, some primitive mould-making (a plastic rubbish bin and a Chinese wok) and a lot of burnt fingers, a new type of production process was invented. In this strange hybrid of industry and craft, the raw material is heated, coloured and pushed and pulled, stretched and bonded to itself, to create new net structures and web shapes. It is an exciting return to the handmade, but this time with a technologically advanced man-made material and a mechanical production process.

Above all, the gratification of being able to manufacture instantly, to be in direct contact with the hot, fresh raw material and to be able to affect the shape through split-second decisions came as a big contrast to the long, drawn-out process that has become an inevitable part of designing for industry.

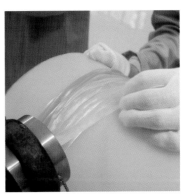

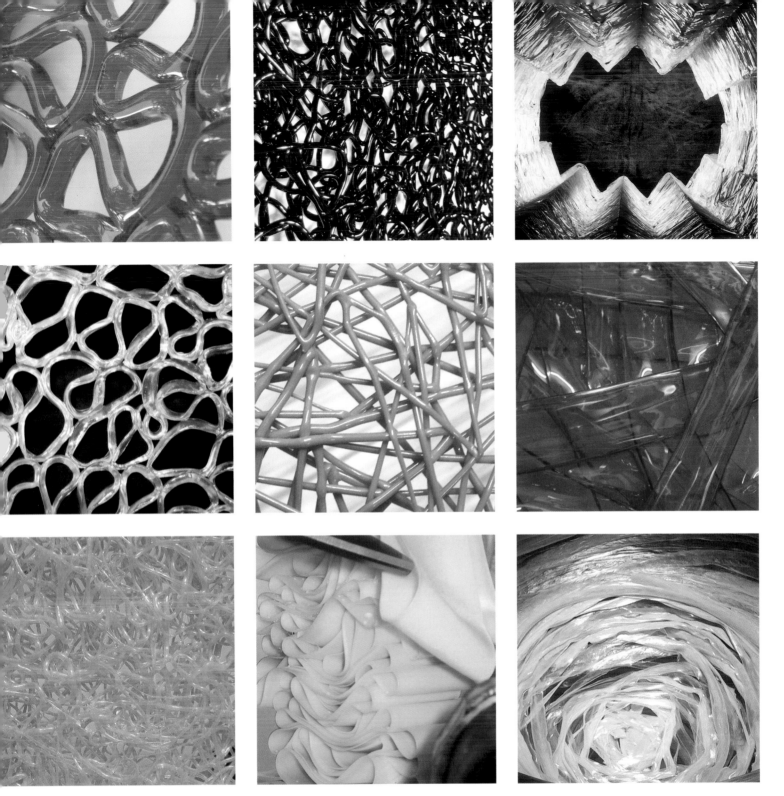

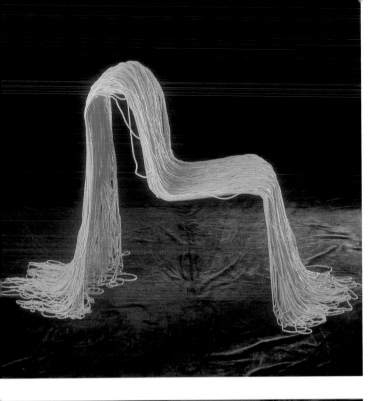

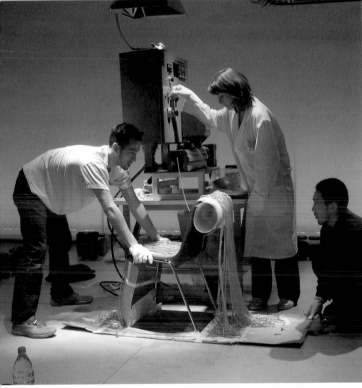

Right and overleaf — I always feel that the product design world underestimates the expressionistic possibilities of materials. How timid and safe is the treatment of the raw substance in product design and architecture, compared with the wild and extravagant beauty that can be found in the world of art. The work of British-based sculptor Anish Kapoor is a perfect example of the love and understanding of materials pushed to their radical conclusions, in colour and texture.

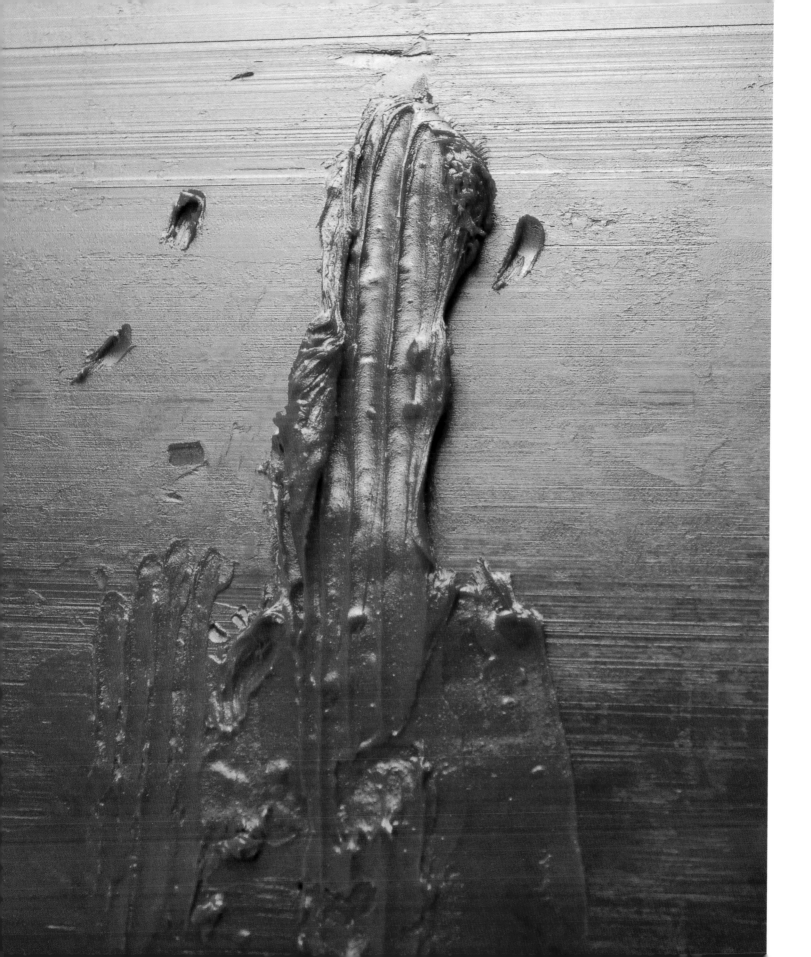

Pages 108 – 133 — The following work by British sculptors
Antony Gormley and David Mach explore the potential in
structure or repetition in materials to produce inspirational works.

To be an effective designer it is essential to be familiar with materials, but it does not end there. If you know nothing of the way those raw materials are put together – how they react under pressure, how they are fixed and folded, riveted, bonded, soldered and spot-welded, pressed and punched, glued or dowelled, woven and knitted – you are going to be handicapped in your adventures in design.

The nature of the modern world means that, as tasks become more and more specialized, aspects of work that used to happen in harmonious coexistence, such as design, engineering and manufacturing, are now separate in their teaching, their practice and, increasingly, their geographic location.

This separation is compounded by the almost total dominance of computers as the primary means of shape-making, which often results in a corresponding lack of integration with the means of production. In the not too distant future, this may not be particularly important, as it could soon be possible for materials to shape themselves to the digital commands of sophisticated programmers. But for the time being there is a distance between the computer-generated images of the fresh-faced design-college graduate and the reality of contemporary manufacturing technology.

The joy of welding —
Luckily for me, I started my career in the pre-virtual world, and my connection with design began a long time after my encounter with the means of construction. From a quick lesson in welding came the discovery of a world of making things without even having to draw them first! The joy of welding, for me, was confirmed through developing the ability to make things that actually stood up. No longer did my primitive constructions collapse when a fatter-than-average punter sat on them.

I was getting faster, too – a new chair every day was not unusual. As I welded deep into the night, I was entranced to have found an inherently flexible and forgiving means of making things that suited my impatient and chaotic nature. The careful planning and rigorous cutting of woodwork were not for me. Nor was the year-long wait for tools to be cut in the Far East, the massive investment required for plastic production or the patience needed to wait for subsequent firings of clay before a pot could be ready. No way.

With welding, a steel bar could be quickly chopped and bent, and then assembled into three-dimensional creations that were so quick to create that it felt like drawing in the round. If it was not to your liking, you just clipped it up, bent it some more and re-welded it. The satisfaction in being able to complete an object within a few hours by mastering a simple manufacturing skill was really what got me hooked. It was this baptism in construction that defined my subsequent disordered emergence as a fully fledged designer.

Man's ingenuity —
I'm guessing that my interest in how things are made and what holds them together was fuelled by the usual boy stuff – Meccano, Lego, taking bicycles to bits. However, I was also fortunate to live, at the age of about six, quite near London's Science Museum. There, laid out in simple, chronological displays, evidence of the development of man's extraordinary ingenuity in processing, assembly and production made an indelible impression on me.

Illustrating this perfectly is the museum's Ships Gallery, where hundreds of immaculate scale models allow you to witness man's massive leaps in imagination over the past three or four thousand years. You see the first primitive boats made of animal hide and twigs, which were followed by simple reed constructions capable of carrying many people and cargo. After this came the harnessing of the wind through innovation in textiles and rigging, and the subsequent highly skilled forming and joining of wood to make increasingly sophisticated ships for more efficient trading, exploration or killing. Then there were the giant leaps forward resulting from the realization that metal also could be made to float. The amazing power of the steam engine was followed by the monster diesel engines that now power ships up to a kilometre (two-thirds of a mile) long. More recently there was the appearance of the new plastics and composite materials that allow for more lightness and rigidity than was ever thought possible.

So there in a single gallery, revealed in minute, miniaturized detail, is the history of the relentless ambition and resourcefulness of humans, powered by their ingenuity in processing new materials. Frankly, it makes me wish I had studied engineering. But lacking that qualification has never stopped me, and I feel that in most people there must lurk an in-built craving to construct things, which should be encouraged and unleashed.

Alienation from production —
I am lucky to be involved in the production process from start to finish. But for most people in the industrialized world this is impossible, and they do not experience the resulting fulfilment. One of the afflictions of modern life is that most people find themselves far removed from the process. This fact has been much documented in the food industry, for instance, whereby some children can no longer recognize even common vegetables. Very few have witnessed the

killing and plucking of a chicken, preferring the antiseptic, clingfilm-clad, skinless breast fillet to anything looking remotely like a bird.

It's a similar situation with clothing. A generation ago fabric sold by the yard was commonplace and people would have the skills necessary to sew or knit their own garments. Within the past decade, however, sewing machines have become as rare as typewriters in the home. Instead, apparel is increasingly manufactured in vast factories in Vietnam or the Philippines using computerized pattern making and cutting. There are even hi-tech factory ships that carry the latest textiles and are ready to respond at the shortest notice to trends and out-of-stocks in the high-street shop.

This lack of understanding of the way things are made is inevitable, given the expansion of mass production and mass consumption in a globalization-mad world. The Wal-Martization of the universe seems unstoppable as the consumer gets greedy for more and more novelty and cheaper and cheaper prices, and is increasingly trained to grow bored and dissatisfied with the current model's performance, shape and colour.

Yet this is not a static state of affairs. Labour costs are never fixed, and the availability of raw materials is clearly not infinite. Also, one can always hope that consumers become more discerning and demand a better quality of product. More importantly, the same force that was instrumental in removing our ability to make things could allow us to take charge again. It is the power of technology.

Revolution in three dimensions —
A revolution has recently taken place in the two-dimensional world of reproducing text and image. Printing has gone from being affordable only in large quantities, through specialist mass producers of print and photographs, to the current situation where it is within easy reach of most, who can produce images, posters, manifestos and even complete novels on their desktops. Now the revolution is set to affect the three-dimensional world. The tools for the production of objects are gradually being put at our disposal through the process of miniaturization and digitalization. It is becoming possible to access processes to make complex artefacts without owning or collaborating with huge plants or industrial complexes.

In fact, in the near future a designer may have access to something that would resemble a medieval village rather than a modern mega-factory. The equivalent of the blacksmith, the leatherworker and the cabinetmaker will be in close proximity, making things or parts of things to measure, and manufacturing and delivering them the same day. The distinction this time around is the automation, digitalization and miniaturization of the processes and equipment. Rapid manufacturing machines, computer-controlled five-axis milling machines and mini aluminium smelters will become increasingly available, sophisticated and adaptable to specific requirements.

The ultimate personalization —
The long-held dream of manufacturers such as Levi Strauss or Smart Car, for made-to-measure jeans or cars assembled in unique specifications to suit the consumer's individual whim, is on the cusp of happening. However, the real revolution will happen as these processes become available to the small company, cooperative or individual, which is then able to design and produce their own garment or vehicle in the way that suits themselves or their local community or consumer.

One only has to look at the music industry to sense the possibility of a flexible, personal and exciting world emerging once more. The liberation of the musician from the restrictions of the megacorp record company, with its fixed constraint of the pressing of records and slow, risky promotion and distribution, has allowed for an explosion of local content, catering to a massively diverse audience.

Just imagine this possibility made accessible to the craftsman, designer or handyman. Everybody will suddenly be free to create their own product to fit a personal need, rather than consuming predetermined, bland goods just because they are cheap. The age of personal constructivism could soon be upon us.

Pages 120 – 123 — Helix models of DNA, the genetic material of most living organisms. Consisting of a large number of nucleotides joined together in single file to form a strand, it demonstrates the underlying structural rules that govern all constructions.

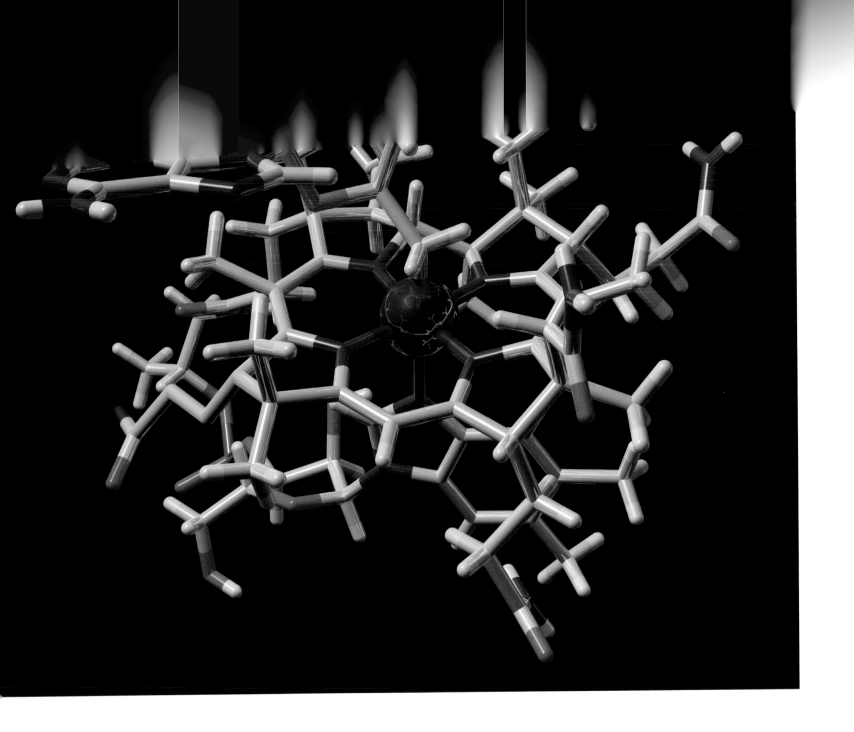

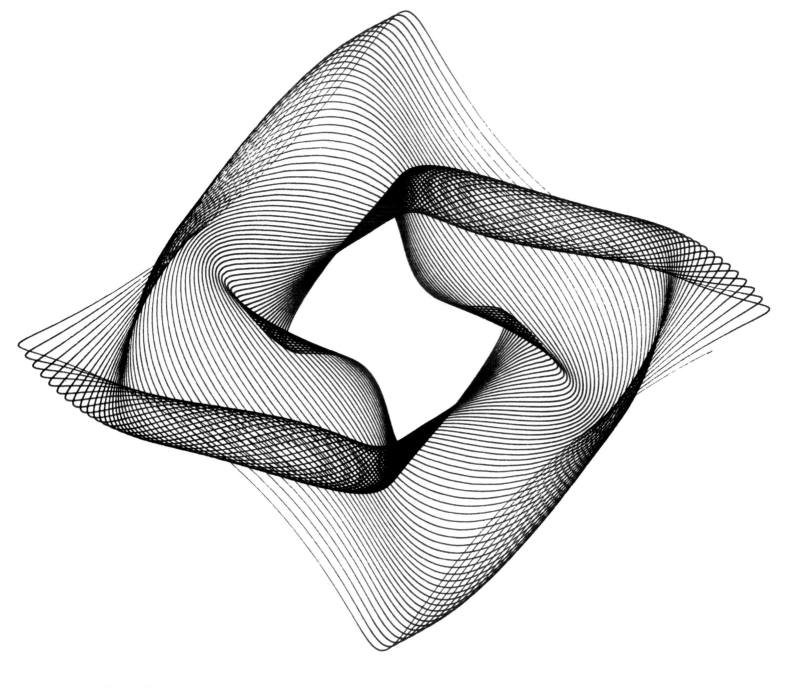

Invented in the 1870s as a means of analysing vibrations, the harmonograph was particularly useful for the study of sound. By the early twentieth century, it was regarded as just a scientific toy for drawing patterns, such as this example, made using a Newton harmonograph of 1909. The device consists of a pen and drawing table mounted on pendulums which are set swinging at right angles to each other. The pen is lowered carefully to the table and traces out the resulting combination of the two vibrations. The pendulums can be made to swing more quickly or slowly by altering the number and position of the weights.

Right — Mathematics, especially geometry, is a recurrent theme of the constructivist design language. This Renaissance illustration by Leonardo da Vinci depicts a polyhedron in which pentagonal (five-sided) and hexagonal (six-sided) sides mesh to form a roughly spherical shape known as a 'truncated icosahedron'. This is akin to the geodesic domes designed in the 1940s and the structure of fulle-rene molecules discovered in the 1990s, as well as the more familiar soccer ball. The illustration was published in Luca Pacioli's *De divina proportione* in 1509.

congruunt duodecim Pentagoni cum viginti Hex.

Unus igitur Trigonicus cum duobus Tetrag
nus efficiunt 4 rectis, & congruunt 20 Trigoni cu

Above and overleaf — The young British sculptor Richard Sweeney is
also influenced by geometry. He exhibited this sculpture installation at the
Cartasia outdoor festival of paper sculpture held in Lucca, Italy, in September
2007. Made from interlocking sheets of paper or cardboard intersecting at
right angles, the paper scale models and large cardboard sculptures explore
the creation of three-dimensional form through series of slices.

Left — During the Renaissance, artists gradually rediscovered and illustrated
the geometric solids described by Archimedes nearly two thousands years
earlier. The German astronomer Johannes Kepler systematically defined the
complete set of so-called Archimedian solids, or 'convex uniform polyhedra',
publishing them in 1619 in his book *Harmonices mundi*. The book set out
Kepler's belief in a universal harmony based on geometry, and it contained
engravings and woodcuts by the skilled engraver Wilhelm Schickard. Some of
these Archimedian solids are shown in this engraving from the book, including
the truncated icosahedron (No. 4) that Da Vinci had illustrated a century
earlier (see page 125).

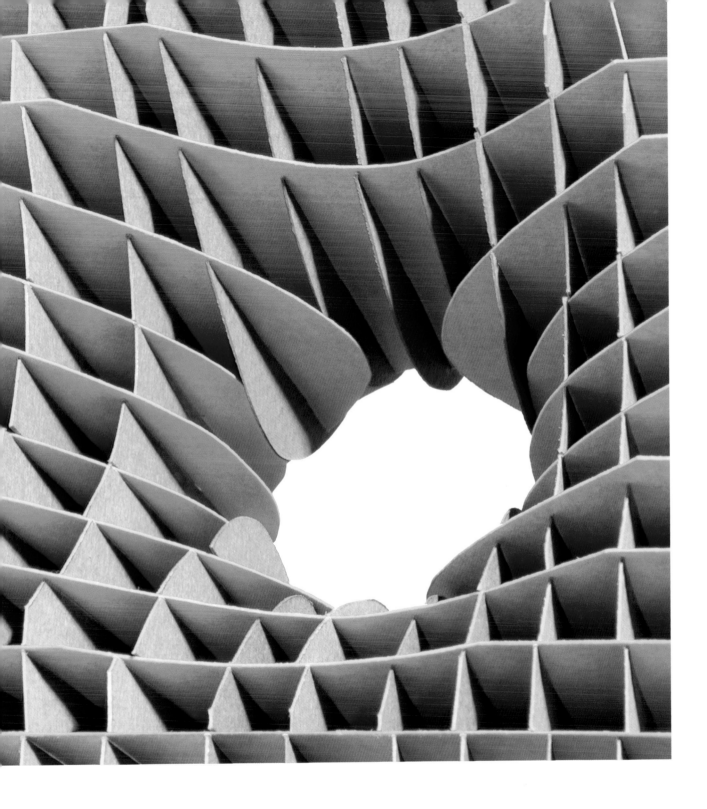

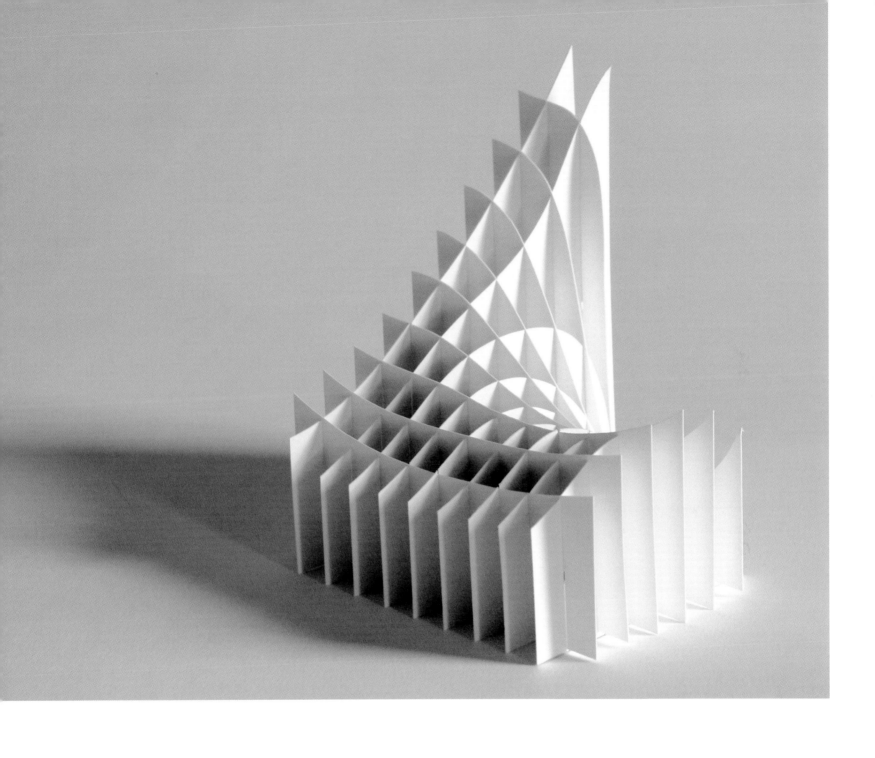

A hornets' nest demonstrates the mathematical
rules that underpin everything around us.

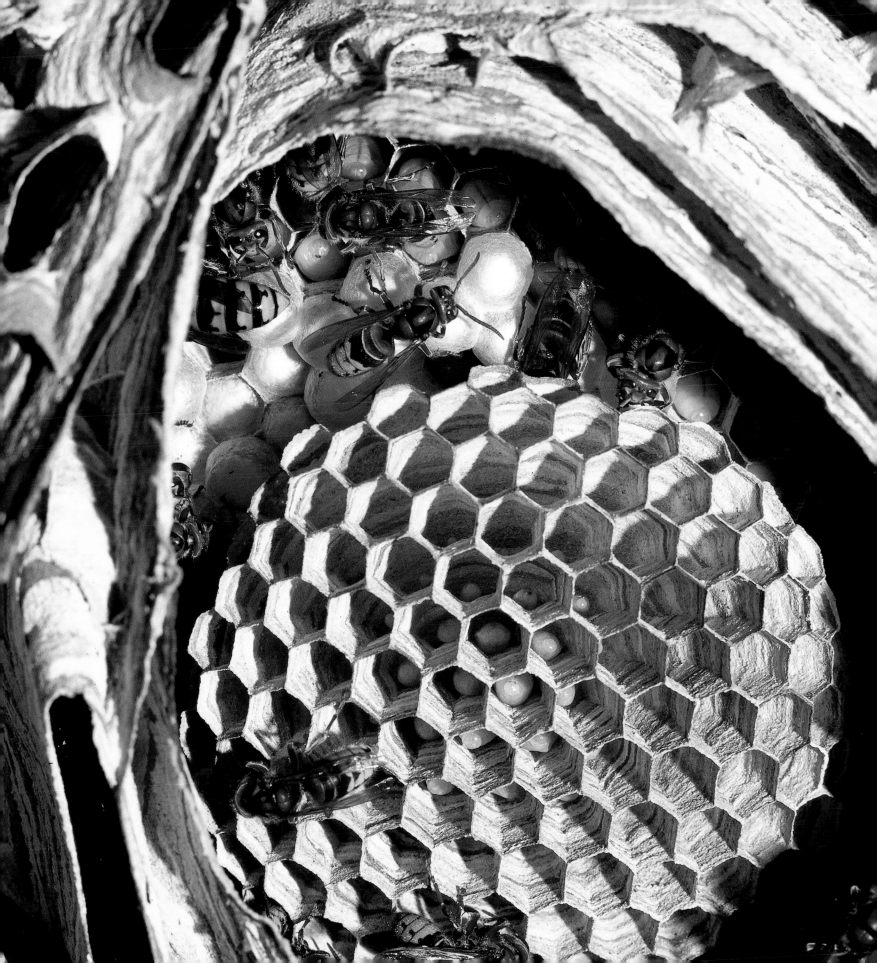

Effective, economical and efficient construction methods are used by animals for their nests.

Clockwise from top left — White storks build their bulky nests of branches, dirt and debris on rooftops, churches, even telephone poles, returning to them year after year – some nests are hundreds of years old. An organ-pipe mud-dauber wasp nest consists of a series of mud tubes resembling organ pipes. Made from interwoven reeds and mud, the nest of the black-breasted weaver has an elaborate entrance tunnel. A southern masked weaver adult male builds its woven-grass nest with a bottom entrance. The common wasp chews wood fibre to build a multi-celled nest with vent holes in the paper-like walls. A harvester ants' nest has multiple levels.

A beaver dam. Beavers build dams in rivers and streams to create ponds in which they can build their lodges. For the dams they use green willow, birch, poplar and driftwood mixed with mud and stones. They also build their lodges from branches and mud, renewing the mud in the autumn, when it hardens in the frost.

Left — Termite mounds in Kakadu National Park in Australia's Northern Territory. Inside each mound is an elaborate network of tunnels and chambers.

The construction processes that feature in Antony Gormley's sculptures bear a striking similarity to the structures on the previous pages.

Traditional Korean monks' shoes, which are made from straw, show extraordinary economy of means. These are from the Jongno area of Seoul.

Right — A lounge chair by the Philippines-based furniture design and manufacturing company Interior Crafts of the Island Inc., managed by the award-winning designer Kenneth Cobonpue. The lounge chair is made from polycotton on a steel frame.

This ship being built by unemployed youngsters at Lelystad, in the Netherlands,
is an example of monumental construction with a natural sophistication.

Left — A vine bridge over a river in western Ivory Coast, West Africa.
These bridges are built entirely of natural materials and are in constant use.

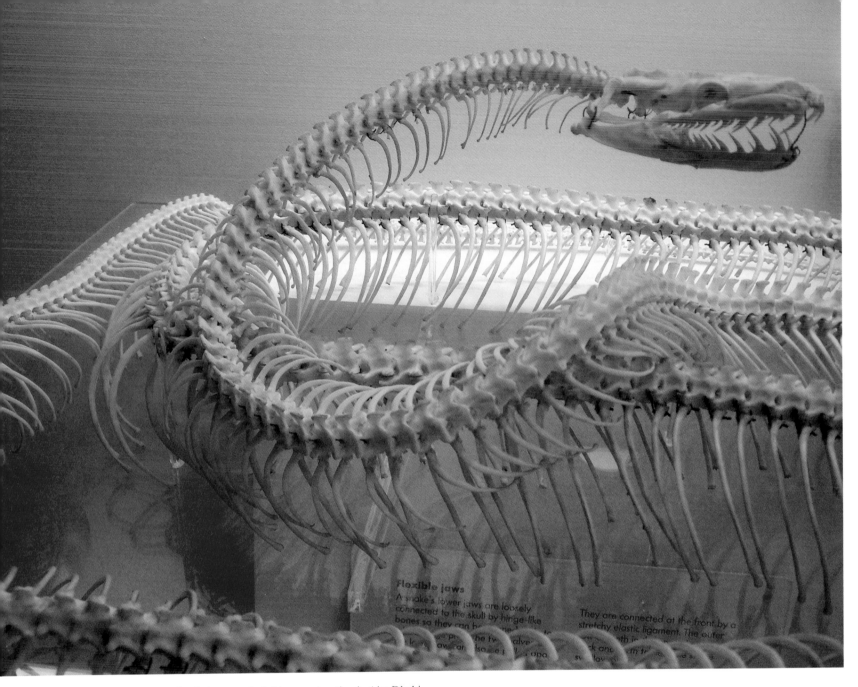

Flexible jaws
A snake's lower jaws are loosely
connected to the skull by hinge-like
bones so they can be opened ...
... the two halves
... awe ... also ... opa

They are connected at the front by a
stretchy elastic ligament. The outer
... with ...
... k and ... m the ... ds.
... sw ...

Above and right — A snake skeleton and a bridge construction in Abu Dhabi –
disparate functionalities, but the same functional need for strength.

142 — 143 Constructivism

Above and right — The transhumant way of life involves moving livestock between grazing grounds, typically from low valleys and desert plains in winter to the high pastures in the summer. This demands highly portable housing that is adaptable to fluctuations in temperature. Here Kazakh herders settle a yurt at a base in Altay Prefecture during the autumn transhumance in Xinjiang Uygur Autonomous Region, northwest China.

Above and right — Also known as the Bird Nest, the National Stadium for the 2008 Olympic Games in Beijing, seen here under construction, shares a visual connection with the Kazakh yurt (see pages 144–5), but has none of its flexibility.

Above and right — The geometrical structure of the National Aquatic Center, or Watercube, for the 2008 Olympic Games in Beijing consists of a lightweight membrane of 4,000 plastic air bubbles resembling water bubbles, intended to make it an energy-efficient insulated greenhouse.

A craftsman weaves a fishing net out of cane in Apulia, southern Italy (left), and a satellite dish (above). Although from drastically different cultures, these lightweight structures share an aesthetic.

Above and right — The geometry of basketmaking and CAD (computer-aided design) models has here been translated into metal furniture.

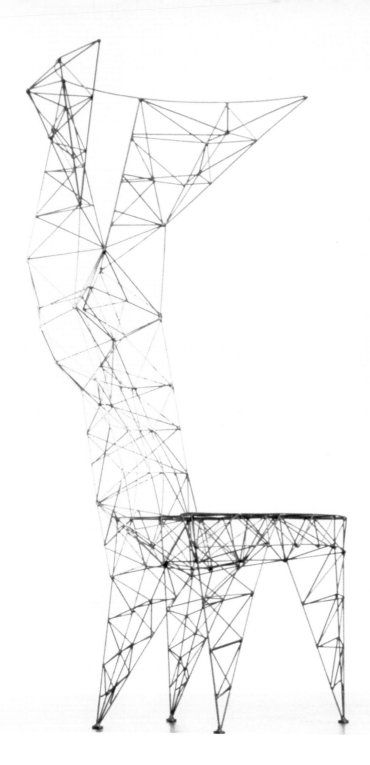

Designed by Jennifer Carpenter at TRUCK product
architecture, the STRETCHfence is a concept project
that reinvents the typical park fence as an on-the-road
rest station for New York cabbies.

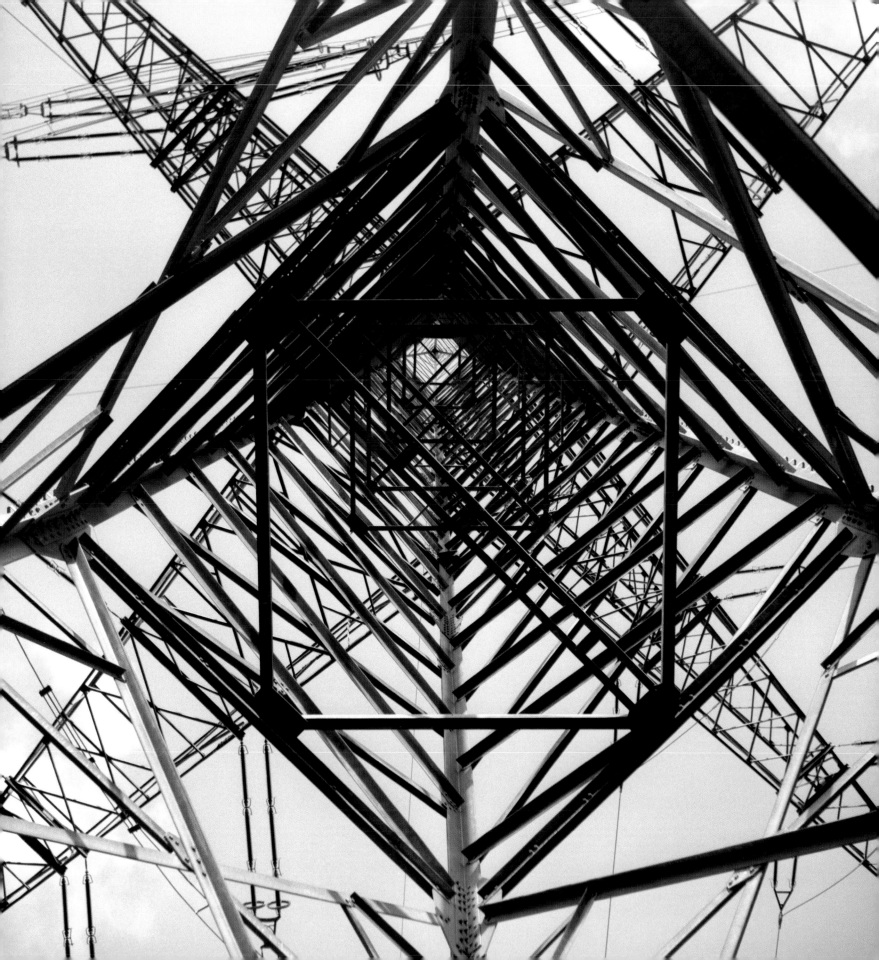

Above and left — Recycled paper and plastic extrusions of pre-consumer waste, from the Finnish industrial giant UPM, form the structure and cladding of the Artek Pavilion. It was designed by the Japanese architect Shigeru Ban for the 2007 Milan Furniture Fair.

The Cafe de Flower, in Seoul, South Korea,
with its multicoloured corrugated facade.

Scaffolding on a building in Indonesia offers a
refreshingly undesigned use of available materials.

Student workshop at the Ball State University where Architecture and Planning students were given 500 pallets as raw material.

Seeking the future of materials —

Design often feels like a business that works in ever-decreasing, self-referential typologies, where often one feels constrained by the limitations of existing materials and methods of building or manufacturing things. Designers therefore need always to be seeking out the cutting edge of experimental technologies in building materials. When a new method of making stuff is discovered, it is the moment when designers can really get to work. Here is a fabulous example which I find inspirational and which hints at all manner of possibilities in the overlapping fields of material technology, invention, environmental protection and architecture.

Wolf Hilbertz was a professor of architecture at the University of Texas when, in the mid-1970s, he began developing a process using electrical current through sea water to grow limestone construction materials underwater. The build-up of limestone created these solid structures. Hilbertz had discovered that, when metal frames were dropped into shallow tropical waters and then connected to very low, safe voltages, dissolved minerals that occur in sea water would be deposited on the metal structures, growing a crust of natural white limestone. He speculated that whole buildings or even complete island communities could eventually be created in the sea.

Subsequently, Hilbertz worked with the coral ecologist Dr Thomas Goreau to adapt the process to coral reef restoration and shore protection. It was found that naturally occurring corals could be encouraged to grow on the steel structures, and their extremely slow growth rates were sped up by three or four times, thanks to the application of electrical current, which could be generated through low-impact technologies such as solar cells or wind power. The new structures were then quickly populated by a wide range of organisms, which included crabs, clams, octopus, lobsters, sea urchins and barnacles, as well as large shoals of fish. As well as regenerating the damaged reef, reintroducing all kinds of endangered sea life could prove an attractive proposition for biotourism. How fabulous is that!

Not only did they succeed in creating a new method of building, but also as a spin-off they created this new material (named Biorock) that has similar properties to concrete yet actually grows rather than being manufactured. Just imagine the infinite, unforeseen possibilities of such an invention – a building material that could be used to create whole buildings or sea defences or fish farms in which the entire infrastructure is grown, and continues to develop throughout its life. Wolf himself dreamed of floating sea towns where people would live in complete harmony with nature. Now that's the kind of constructivism to aspire to!

Fastenings are all too often ignored in the
larger scheme of things but play an inordinately
important role.

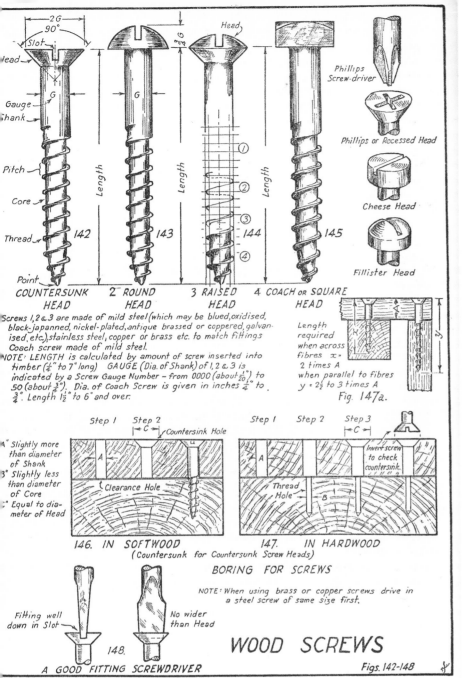

2 G
90°
Slot
Head
Gauge
Shank
Pitch
Core
Thread
Point

142
COUNTERSUNK HEAD

2 ROUND HEAD 143
G
Length

3 RAISED HEAD 144
Head
① ② ③ ④
Length

4 COACH OR SQUARE HEAD 145
Length

Phillips Screw-driver

Phillips or Recessed Head

Cheese Head

Fillister Head

Screws 1, 2 & 3 are made of mild steel (which may be blued, oxidised, black-japanned, nickel-plated, antique brassed or coppered, galvanised, etc.), stainless steel, copper or brass etc. to match fittings. Coach screw made of mild steel.

NOTE: LENGTH is calculated by amount of screw inserted into timber ($\frac{1}{4}$" to 7" long). GAUGE (Dia. of Shank) of 1, 2 & 3 is indicated by a Screw Gauge Number – from 0000 (about $\frac{1}{20}$") to 50 (about $\frac{3}{4}$"). Dia. of Coach Screw is given in inches $\frac{1}{4}$" to $\frac{3}{4}$". Length $1\frac{1}{2}$" to 6" and over.

Length required when across fibres $x =$ 2 times A
when parallel to fibres $y = 2\frac{1}{2}$ to 3 times A

Fig. 147a.

Step 1   Step 2
C
Countersink Hole
A
Clearance Hole

A" Slightly more than diameter of Shank
B" Slightly less than diameter of Core
C" Equal to diameter of Head

146. IN SOFTWOOD

Step 1   Step 2   Step 3
C
Invert screw to check countersink.
A
Thread Hole
B

147. IN HARDWOOD
(Countersunk for Countersunk Screw Heads)

BORING FOR SCREWS

NOTE: When using brass or copper screws drive in a steel screw of same size first.

Fitting well down in Slot

No wider than Head

148.
A GOOD FITTING SCREWDRIVER

WOOD SCREWS

Figs. 142-148

PLATE 27.

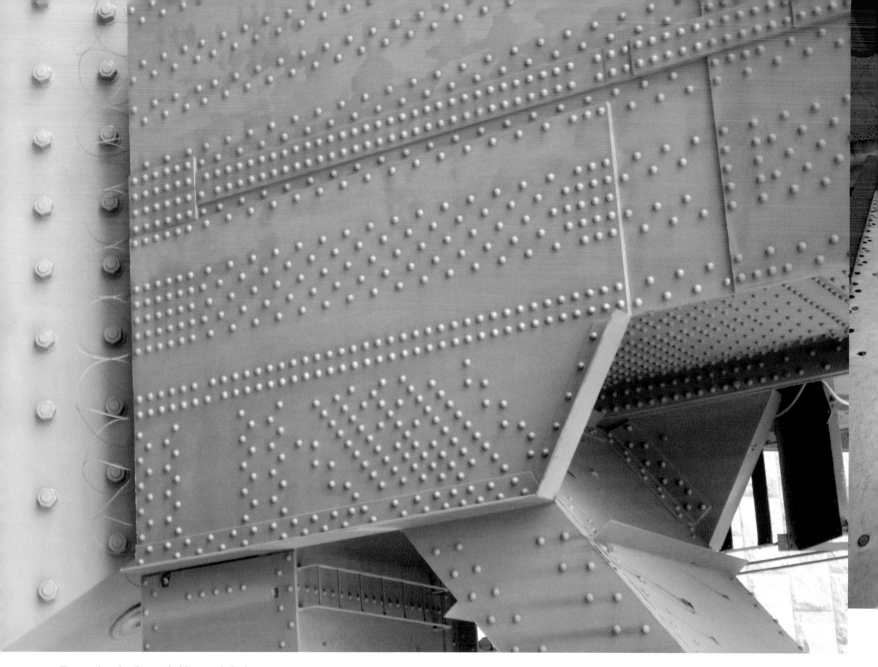

Expressive riveting on bridges and airplanes –
no decoration needed.

Above — Extraordinary longevity from the simplest of
constructions, at England's 4,000-year-old Stonehenge.

The labyrinthine installation entitled 'Embankment', by British artist Rachel Whiteread, was enormous enough to fill the monumental space of the Turbine Hall of London's Tate Modern art gallery.

Around 14,0000 casts of the insides of different boxes were stacked up to form Rachel Whiteread's installation at the Tate Modern's Turbine Hall.

US artist John Powers's 'Voluntaries #16' was part of a series of 23 installations shown in a 2005 solo exhibition in New York. Each piece contained 1,000 blocks.

Right — Spacers used in kilns to adjust the height of shelves,
allowing good heat flow around the work being fired.

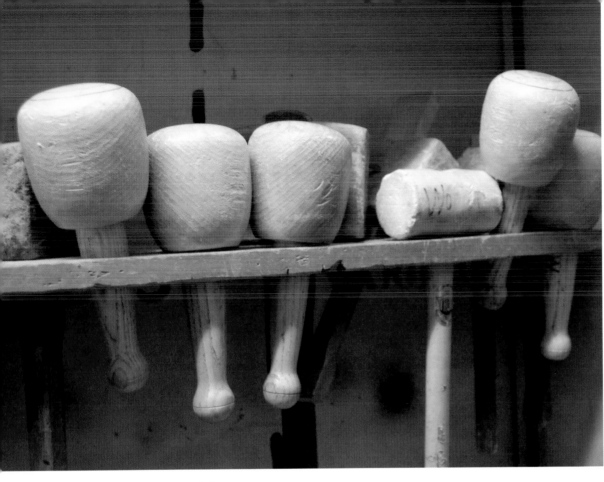

Above and right — The tools define
the construction methods.

Left — Man hammering iron spheres on an anvil, 1497. Woodcut from *Hortus Sanitatis* 'Garden of Health', printed in Strasbourg by Johann Prüss in 1497.

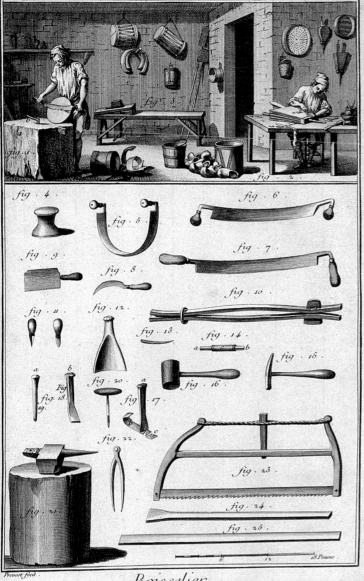

fig. 3

fig. 1

fig. 2

fig. 4

fig. 5

fig. 6

fig. 9

fig. 7

fig. 8

fig. 10

fig. 11

fig. 12

fig. 13

fig. 14

a   b

fig. 15

Fig

fig. 18

a   b

fig. 20

a

fig. 16

19

fig. 17

c

fig. 22

fig. 23

fig. 21

fig. 24

fig. 25

6   12   18 Pouces.

Prevost fecit.

Boisselier.

Woodcut illustration by Jost Amman (1539–1591) from *De Omnibus Illiberalibus Siue Mechanicis Artibus ... Liber* by Hartmann Schopper (b.1542), published in Germany, 1574. One of 133 woodcuts from Schopper's book, written in Latin, which detailed a variety of trades, this shows printers in a workshop. Two men in the foreground are depicted inking type and preparing paper on a printing press, while in the background men are seen selecting and setting the type to be printed.

Left — Illustrations on how to use a wood saw to cut properly and how to construct a dovetail joint.

Right — The methods of construction will always influence the final form.

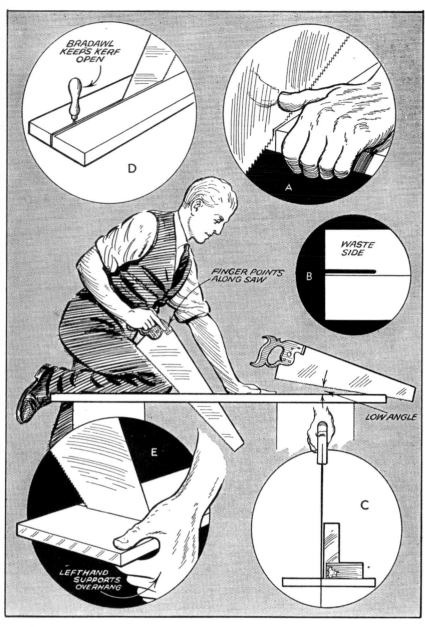

FIG. 1. POINTS TO FOLLOW WHEN USING THE HANDSAW

A. Starting the cut, the saw bearing against the left thumb. B. How saw cut is usually on waste side of line. C. Guide to holding the saw upright. D. Preventing wood from binding on saw. E. Supporting overhang on completion of cut.

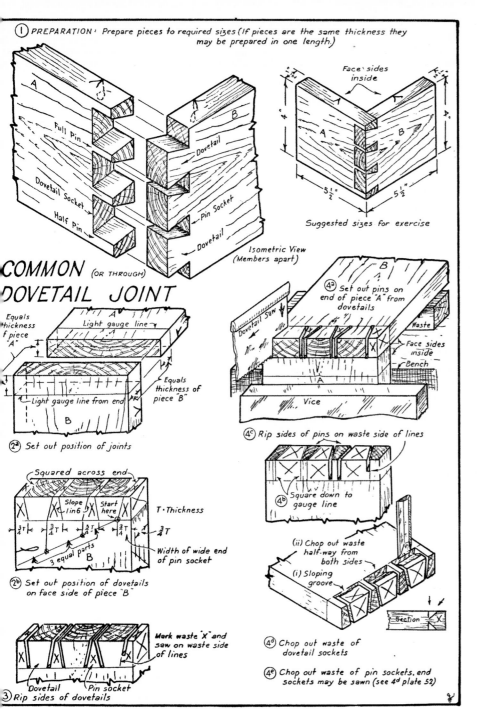

① PREPARATION: Prepare pieces to required sizes (If pieces are the same thickness they may be prepared in one length.)

A

Full Pin

Dovetail Socket

Half Pin

Dovetail

Pin Socket

Dovetail

B

Isometric View
(Members apart)

Face sides inside

A   B

4"   4"

5½"   5½"

Suggested sizes for exercise

COMMON (OR THROUGH)
DOVETAIL JOINT

Equals thickness f piece "A"

Light gauge line

A

Equals thickness of piece "B"

Light gauge line from end

B

② Set out position of joints

Squared across end

Slope 1 in 6   Start here

X   X   X   X

¾T   ¾T   ¾T   ¾T

3 equal parts

B

T·Thickness

Width of wide end of pin socket

②ᵇ Set out position of dovetails on face side of piece "B"

X   X   X

X   X   X

Dovetail   Pin socket

Mark waste "X" and saw on waste side of lines

③ Rip sides of dovetails

④ᵃ Set out pins on end of piece "A" from dovetails

B

Dovetail Saw

Waste

Face sides inside

Bench

A

Vice

④ᶜ Rip sides of pins on waste side of lines

④ᵇ Square down to gauge line

(ii) Chop out waste half-way from both sides

(i) Sloping groove

Section   X

④ᵈ Chop out waste of dovetail sockets

④ᵉ Chop out waste of pin sockets, end sockets may be sawn (see 4ᵈ plate 52)

Above — Piles of Lithuanian timber at the sawmill awaiting
secondary processing – the factory as a source of inspiration.

Rough-sawn blanks awaiting
conversion to parquet flooring.

Assembly and quality control line.

Patterns for chair components.

Moulds for plywood pressing.

Stacks of chairs awaiting finishing.

British designer Peter Marigold's Make/Shift shelving system, which expands and contracts to fill different-sized spaces. The system comes in a variety of materials.

Wood installations at a design event in Seoul, South Korea.
Seo You-Rim (left); 'Spread Out' by Lee Sam Woong
(centre and right) made out of ashwood.

Left — Glass blowing at the Dartington Crystal factory in Devon, UK.

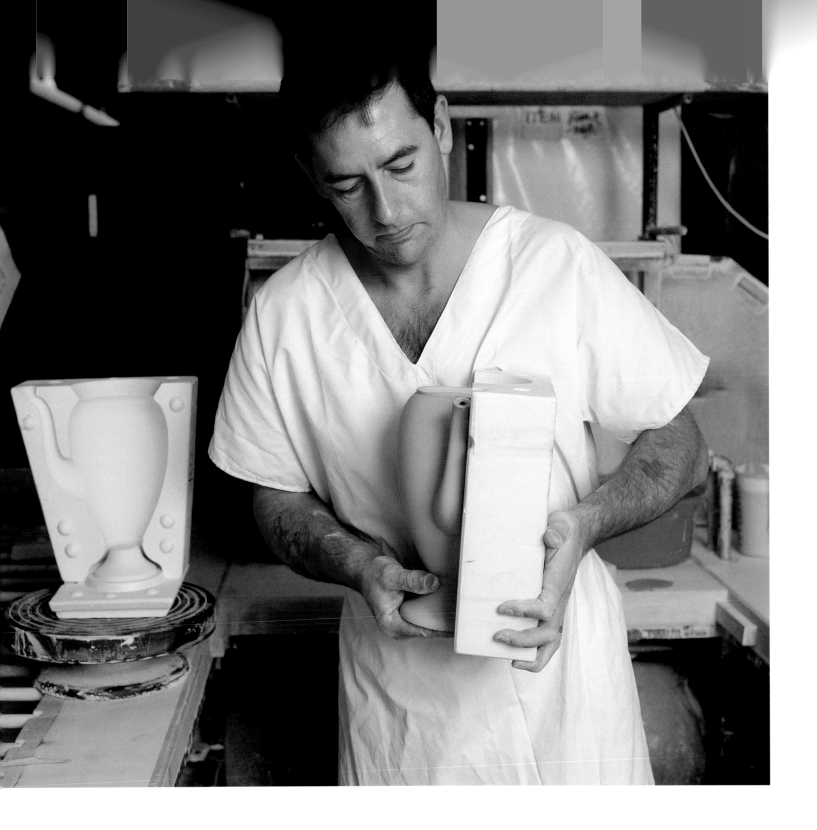

Left — Kiln for firing pottery.

Right — Mould for slip-casting.

The rotational moulding process, a relatively crude method of moulding, forces the designer to acknowledge the limitations of the production process.

Above and right — Car headlamp factories
with an impressive array of hi-tech and low-tech
production techniques.

Highly technical metal deposition
techniques and robot finishing arms.

The Industrial Revolution was powered by
industrial methods of cast-iron production, almost
unchanged to this day.

Left and right — New production methods will allow us to produce unforeseen objects using laser cutting and extrusion.

Above and right — Industrial plastic extrusion and
blown film extrusion.

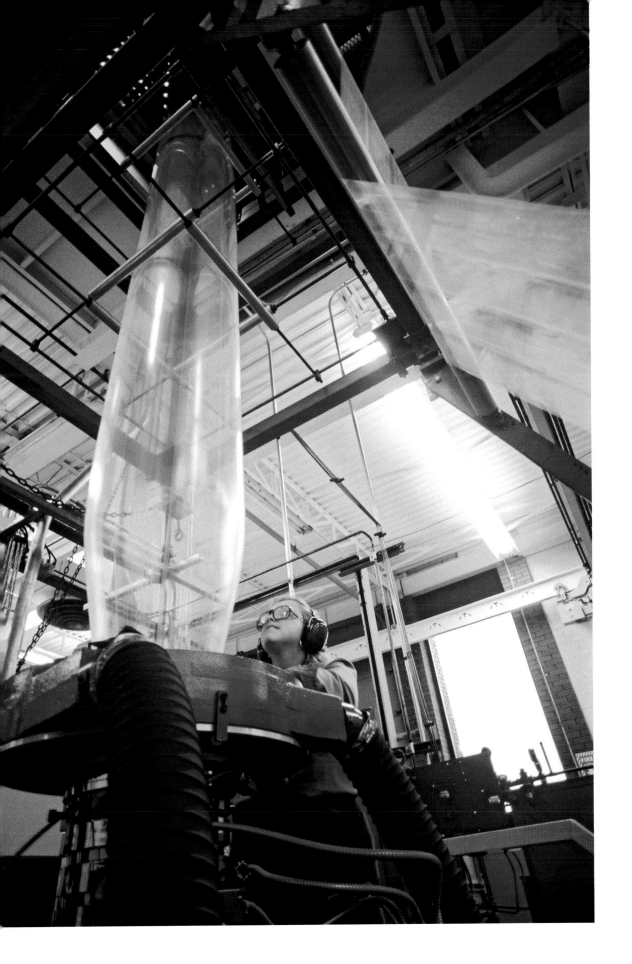

The public used to be familiar with construction methods through exposure to the blacksmith shop and the local cabinet-maker. Now that industrial production is the norm, modern processes are largely invisible.

An urge to decorate and adorn remains one of the unique features of the human race. Is this something to be repressed, or should it simply be reassessed against the backdrop of modern times?

No matter which culture or what period or ethnic group you choose, the glory of pattern has been ever-present in its many guises. The impulse to decorate and adorn happens very early on in the development of humans, yet it appears to be superfluous. Almost everything else can be explained by natural selection, but not making useless patterns, adorning things or making yourself more beautiful. Palaeontologists know that Neolithic man was already using pigments and scratching regular markings into bone tools as early as 100,000 years ago. Whether this was a form of worship, a method of personalization, an assertion of ownership or simply a way to enhance their surroundings, we can only speculate – so speculate I will!

Intrinsic pattern and texture —
For me, decoration is omnipresent, whether hidden in the smallest detail or so blatantly present that we scarcely notice it any more. I can't walk down even the dullest, most banal street without noticing the richness of texture and the often unconscious use of pattern. Texture and pattern emerge from each course of paving stone, the cast-iron grating, the granite kerbstone with mottled and hammered surfaces, the drain cover textured with raised lettering to create a non-slip surface. And this is just a description of a short walk along a local street with my eyes firmly fixed on the ground. As I lift my eyes to behold the vertical repeat patterns of fences and the diamonds of wire mesh, I notice the regular piercing of window frames, themselves subdivided into smaller grids in multiples of twos, fours and sixes, and the cladding of warehouses with rolled aluminium or corrugated galvanized steel.

When I look even closer, the decorative nature of things that were presumably intended to be purely functional is revealed, from the imprint of the wooden shuttering on the columns of a motorway bridge to the diamond pattern of security grilles. I notice the regular arrangements that exist to reinforce structure, such as the laying of brickwork in all types of configurations, the welded fillets on a lamppost or the regular, overlapping planks and scratchy tar-paper roofs of garden sheds. There is such variety and complexity layered in something as banal as road surfacing. Although these constructions may well have a basis in sound engineering practice, it is clear that a lot of care and pride has been expended in their placing and layout. Therein may lie some of the reasons for the human predisposition to decorate.

Universal forms —
An ability to apply order and rhythm to raw materials and make regular and repeat interventions to build stronger constructions must have helped to power

the development of humankind. No wonder, then, that decoration shares roots with mathematics, nature and science. As you dig deeper into the history of ornamentation, you start spotting a series of constants that are also present in geometry, physics and even chemistry. Spirals, grids, spheres, chains, cubes, stripes, branches, pyramids, tessellations, hexagons – all appear and reappear in widely disparate cultures during different periods of history. I'm very interested in the root of pattern, coming from the patterns found in molecular science and mathematics. Cell structures and molecules are the repeat patterns that form the building blocks of our whole universe, so maybe we are just reflecting our own make-up and that of the world around us.

Rejecting ornament —
I have always felt comfortable with the practice of exposing intrinsic structures to form decoration. To reveal and enhance the workings and the construction of an object to expressive effect seems right. But decoration just for the sake of it? That's another story altogether.

In modern times, efforts have been made to question the existence of ornamentation and embellishment, and many attempts have been made to eradicate it completely – with mixed success. Designers and architects have been in an almost constant state of denial about the legitimacy of decoration and pattern for the best part of a century. In 1908 the Austro-Hungarian architect Adolf Loos famously pronounced ornament to be superfluous, a crime, degenerate and, worse still, immoral! By the 1920s, after the architect Walter Gropius had involved Germany's Bauhaus, the faith in radically simplified forms and functionality, underpinned by the idea that mass production was the goal, meant that decoration got short shrift from the elite and the opinion-formers. Against this puritanical machine-age backdrop, using decoration has always felt like a guilty pleasure for any contemporary designer. It can be argued that in the modern world pattern is no longer needed and ornamentation can be rejected – but try as its opponents might, it inevitably creeps back.

The more I look at the work of contemporary enthusiasts for minimalism, the more I see a series of closet pattern-makers. Whatever the attempts to eradicate it, even ardent modernists find themselves carefully detailing the exterior

cladding of their building in a regular pattern, or within the architecture itself defining the rhythm used for the spacing of structural elements or the perspective.

For the public good —
It strikes me that figurative decoration, as opposed to the structural decoration just described, must have its origins in the sharing of information. So although we might argue about the function that cave drawings of a hunting scene had – whether the purpose was religion or teaching or mere boasting – we can agree that it was for the purpose of communication in a preliterate world. In this context of information sharing, maybe the contemporary designer can feel once more legitimate in his urge to ornament.

If I were once again to walk my street with this attitude, what a revelation. There is the graphic black and white of bicycle lanes and pedestrian crossings, and the primary-colour gaudiness of red stop signs, the omnipresent double yellow lines that now so dominate the landscape, the reflective blue motorway signs and the non-stop luminous pop art flashing of traffic lights – all this decor, and all in the name of communication.

The layer of government-imposed statutory signage is now so familiar that one completely forgets to register its presence at all. Take a moment to notice just that single, supposedly functional human intervention. Its only official role is to prevent accidents, yet, if looked at it in terms of pattern, it is so rich, so dense, so colourful and joyful, that it could almost be recast as government-funded public art.

If we considered decoration as a form of communication that is expressing the surface or the characteristics of an object, interior or building, then perhaps even the ardent minimalist might find slightly less moral delinquency in expressionism. But now we have look to the modern dilemma.

The opposite extreme —
Technology (the machine), which was once used as a means to justify the absence of pattern, is now so versatile, and the application of colour in printed, embroidered, transfer or sprayed form is so affordable, that a crazed resurgence of deco-ration has become a feature of the digital age. Because we *can*, then inevitably we *do* cover any surface that moves with intricate silhouettes of

flowers, gaudy stripes or lurid graphics. In a cyclical challenge to a period when good taste dictated that things should be pale, minimalistic and restrained in form, the pendulum has swung to the opposite side. Graphic artists, textile designers and architects are now intent on covering every conceivable surface in multiple designs.

It is also a fact that, as synthetic materials increasingly rule the world, the need for artifice in texture and colour has correspondingly increased. When materials no longer have an intrinsic identity, designers, scientists and manufacturers feel the inclination to compensate by dyeing, spraying, stippling, spotting, wood-graining and generally roughing up any chemical goo that they are currently using, to try to create, or recreate, an identity for their new artificial wonder material.

The effect is compounded by the newest breakthroughs in manufacturing. Previously the limitations of technology and materials meant that objects or buildings were a certain shape because of the constraints of, say, an injection moulding tool, or an aluminium casting pattern, or engineer's lathe and milling machine. Suddenly this is no longer the case, given the extraordinary developments in rapid manufacturing. These are starting to open the floodgates of unlimited and unconstrained form, with all the potential for free expression and the potential abuse that this new-found liberty will bring.

This is a graphical representation of a mathematical equation. Fractals are often compared to the shapes found in nature because they share a repeating organic pattern. The natural world can only leave any pattern-maker or ornamentalist furious with jealousy.

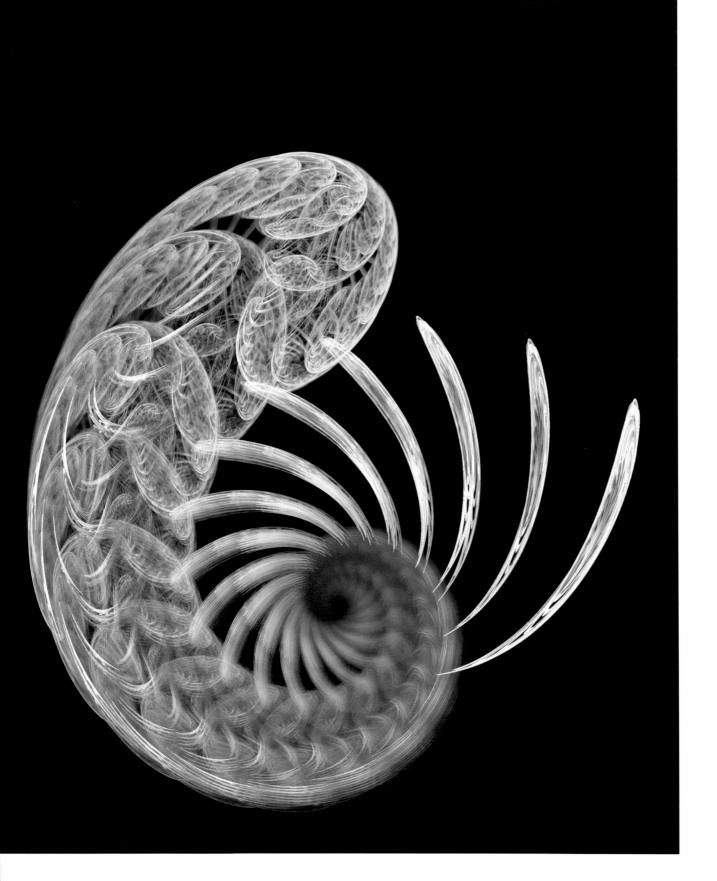

Universal laws of physics and engineering underpin perceived
beauty, in this case York Minster in northern England.

Left — Snowflakes are symmetrical ice crystals that form
in calm air at temperatures near the freezing point of water.
The exact shape of a snowflake depends on local climatic
conditions. No two snowflakes are identical, as each experiences
a wide range of conditions as it forms inside a cloud.

Tord Boontje's 'Blossom' for Swarovski. So often, man-made artefacts seek inspiration from nature.

Above and right — Decorative
tiling and growth patterns share
an underlying geometry.

Above and left — There is so much to be gained
from an understanding of how nature works.

Above and right — Seems as if everybody needs to leave their mark. These handprints made in ochre, from Kakadu National Park, Northern Territory, are one of the oldest forms of Aboriginal rock art in Australia.

Whether for status, for pleasure or for information, mark-making has a place in every society. These Late Palaeolithic Azilian painted pebbles are from the cave of Le Mas d'Azil in France.

Ceramic art is the oldest form of artistic expression, and even prehistoric pottery such as these examples could be intricately decorated.

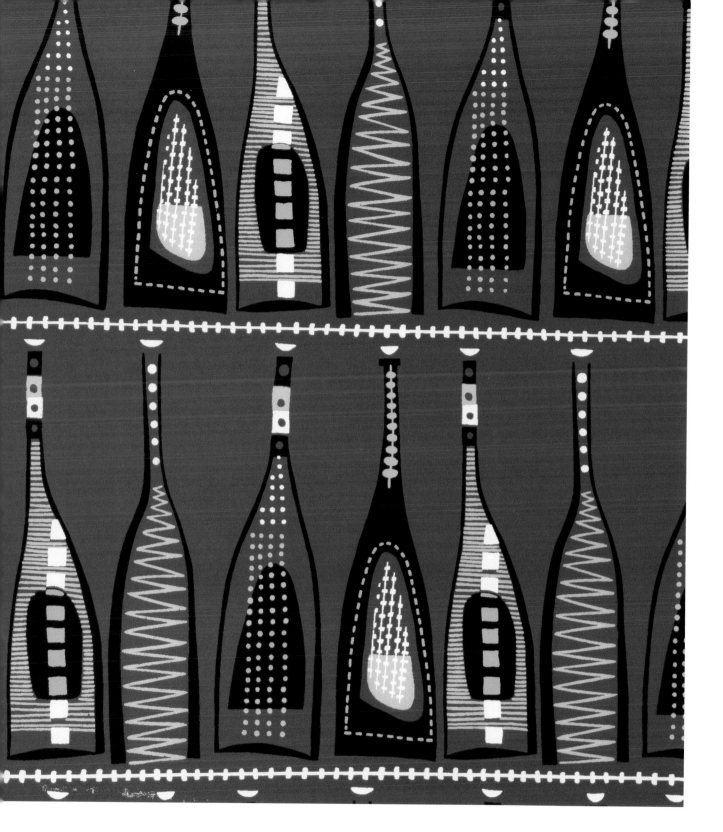

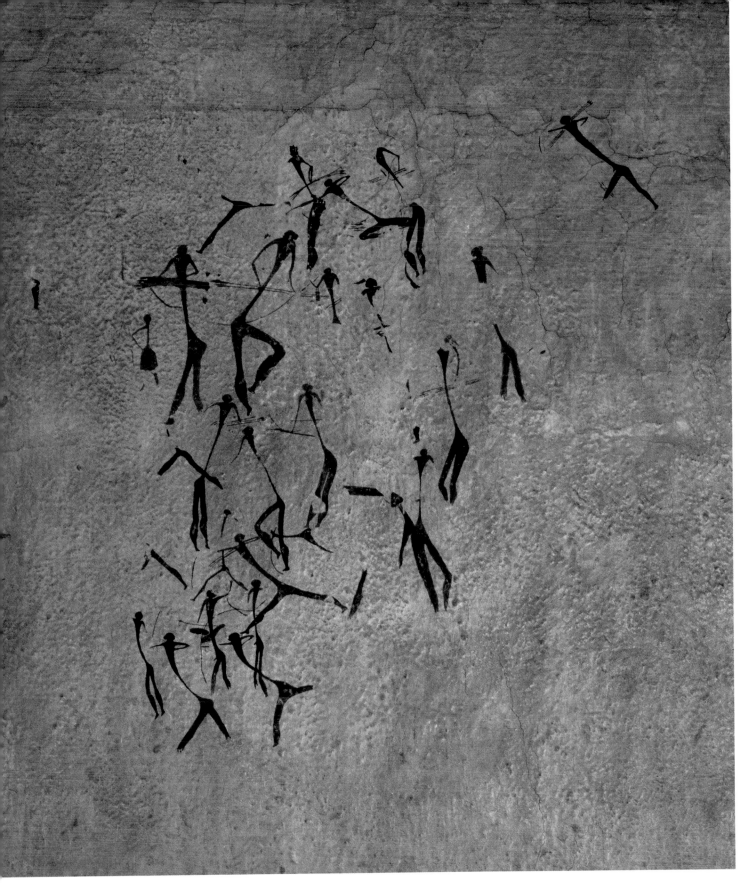

Whether these rock paintings were boasts, advertisements, decoration or sources of information we will never know, but they do not lose their power to amaze. This prehistoric rock painting of bison, *c.*17,000 BCE, is from caves in Lascaux, France.

Left — Carved figure, early Bronze Age, 2700–1900BC (bone) Cypriot.

Right — Pot in the form of a head of Tezcatlipoca, c.1500 (fired clay and paint) Aztec.

Neolithic vase with incised decoration,
2300–1700 BCE, from Fontbouisse, France.

An anthropomorphic carved basalt monolith, possibly sixteenth
century, from the Ejagham (Ekoi) peoples of Cross River State
in southeast Nigeria.

Above — Gourd vessel, reddish brown with incised
design and lateral spout.

Left — Tea disks, taken at Hong da won, tea supplies
shop in Samcheong-dong, Seoul, South Korea.

Above and left — A powerful urge to
self-expression means that even personal
pain is no barrier.

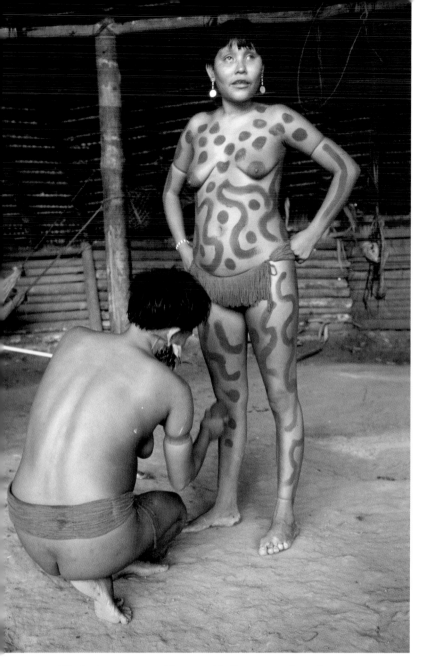

The body as canvas: a Yanomami Indian woman from the
Amazon rainforest paints another woman with *urucu*, a red
paste obtained from seed pods.

Right — A pygmy girl decorated with white designs during
a menstrual ceremony in the Ituri Rainforest of the Democratic
Republic of the Congo.

Above and left — Apparel as a means of reinvention.

Pages 270 – 273 — Disparate cultures sometimes share a common approach.

Left — Woman at a tribal ritual known as a 'sing-sing', when people paint themselves and dress up to represent birds, trees or mountain spirits, in Papua New Guinea.

Right — A finely tattooed Maori in New Zealand.

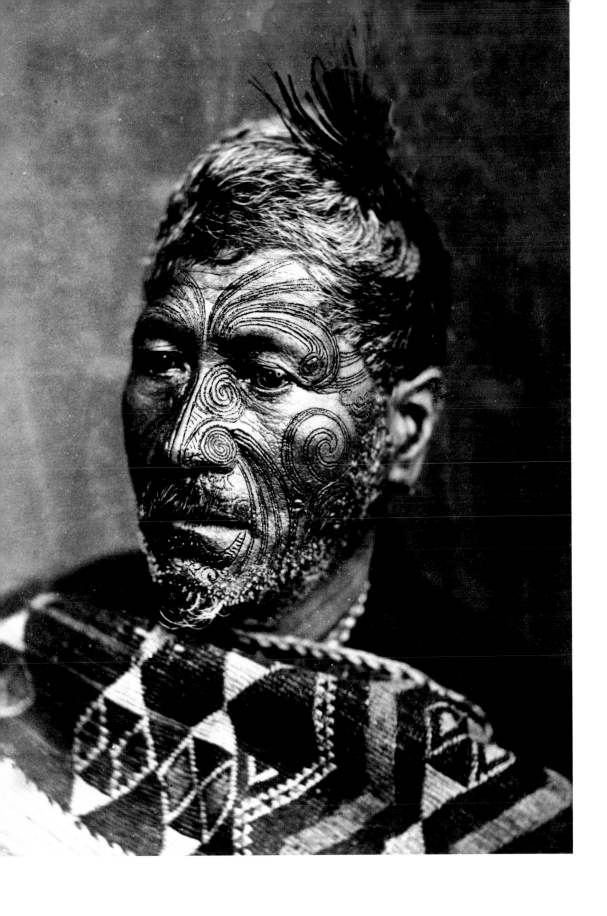

Pages 274 – 279 — Leaving a permanant mark seems to be part of the human condition.

निवेदक

...ीश चन्द

...ारी / सम्मानित गृह...

14 विधान सभा क्षे...

...ोमी

Above — A decorated railway arch shows embellishment
working hard in humble circumstances.

Left — An Islamic meeting and educational house in the
UK that has been decorated with Islamic architectural forms.

Above and right — Cacti and spirals, flames and bubbles
demonstrate little logic or formality, but a huge enthusiasm
for colour, in Brighton, England.

Colour as means of identification.

Above and right — Decorative Buddha
statues in Chiang Mai, Thailand.

Examples of decorative commercial areas.

A textile business in India.

With its distinctive onion domes, the sixteenth-century Cathedral of St Basil in Moscow is a riot of colour and shape that would be perfectly at home in Disneyland.

Above and right — Temporary structures at the annual Burning Man festival held in Nevada's Black Rock desert. Such complexity in a building that will exist for only a week.

Left — Beauty and majesty from the basest of materials, in the ultimate sandcastle competition at Rye on the Mornington Peninsula, Port Phillip Bay, Victoria, Australia.

Right — The Golden Boulder. The granite boulder, covered in gold leaf and topped with a 5.5m (18ft) pagoda, is a Buddhist pilgrimage site on Mount Kyaiktiyo in Burma.

Above and right — Structure and decor interwoven in an Indian palace.

Natural limestone columns in a Vietnamese grotto, Halong Bay.

Obsessive self-expression — The Watts Towers

There are so many examples of adornment and decorative initiative in the world that it is always hard to know where to start, but the examples I always favour are from obsessive decorators – by this I mean people who really couldn't help themselves, who couldn't hold back from building and decorating things.

A good example is Simon Rodia, an Italian immigrant working in South Beach, California, who began working on some towers in 1921 from scrap pipe, wire mesh, old bedsteads and scraps of ceramic from a nearby pottery that were embedded into mortar on the skeletal structures. He laboured on the project until 1954, sometimes walking 30km (20 miles) to find materials. Using nothing more than window-cleaning ladders and hand tools, he built 17 towers, some soaring 30m (99ft) into the air. Rodia is quoted as saying, 'I had in mind to build something big, so I did.' Obviously a man of few words. He was subjected to abuse from locals, some of them suspecting that he was using the towers as antennae to communicate with the Japanese forces during World War II. The towers were subject to a demolition order in 1959 by the hostile local government, but were eventually saved by local enthusiasts of the landmark.

That extraordinary story of an untutored, self-propelled and obsessive need to express a personal vision is by no means unique. Another fabulous tale that always inspires me is the story of the humble French *facteur* ('postman') Ferdinand Cheval. At the advanced age of 43, when he was on his postal round one day in 1879 in Hauterives, Drôme, in south-eastern France, *facteur* Cheval stumbled on an attractive stone – and was moved to build the castle of his childhood dreams. He set about picking up stones on his 33-km (20-mile) round during the day, and building grottoes and towers from them at night. With no training as an architect or artist, he built more than a thousand miniature temples, all incorporated into an edifice 6–11m (20–36ft) high, with a perimeter of 78m (256ft). It was completed in 1912, and he then spent a further eight years building his tomb in the nearby cemetery. Although initially ridiculed, the castle is now listed as a national monument, and is the main source of income for the local town.

This may well be considered folk art, or even the product of a disturbed mind, but for me it is an inspirational example of the intrinsic power of creativity, and of an ability we all possess but too seldom use.

Pages 314 – 327 — Every culture in every era exhibits the propensity for decorative embellishment.

Above and right — Similar arrangements in the pursuit of order, functionality and visual appeal can be found across a broad spectrum, from Italian marble flooring to Korean fish drying.

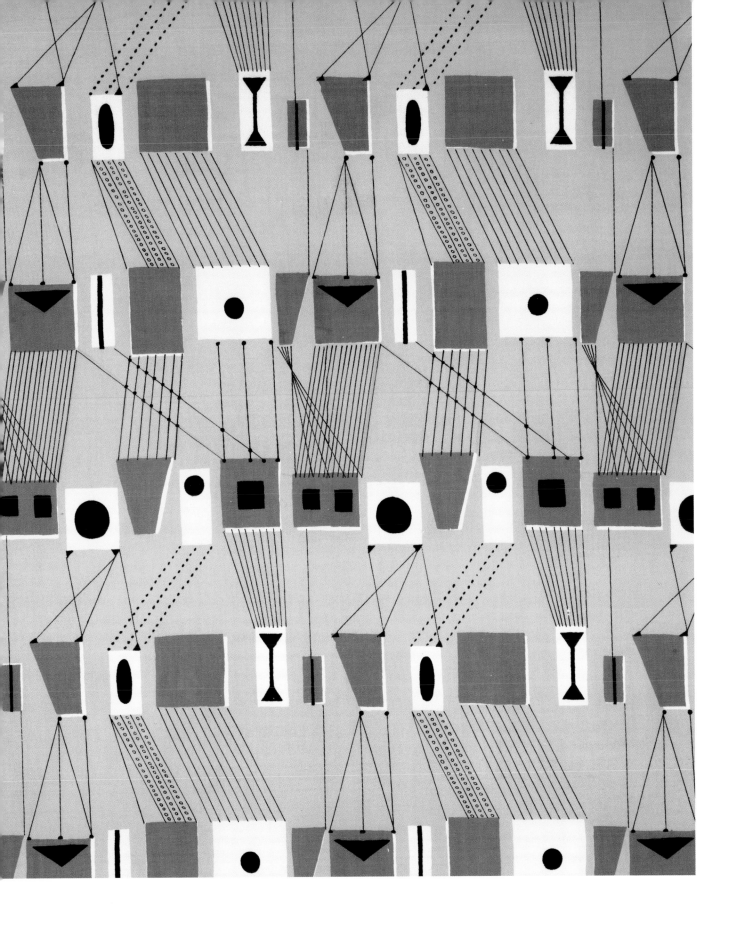

Pages 328 – 335 — The role of fashion, taste, religion and status is of
extreme relevance and is seldom talked about in a design context.

Craft over decoration.

Celestial musicians in Yungang Buddhist grottoes
in Yungang, Shanxi, China.

Art Deco.

The painted dome ceiling at the V&A museum, London, UK.

Above — El Palácio Nacional de Sintra, Portugal.

Left — Interior of the restored Shell Grotto built by the Hanbury
family, in Pontypool, Wales.

Left — A store interior by the New York-based designer Karim Rashid, showing computer-generated imagery.

Right — A guitar store papered with clippings from music magazines.

79

Glass vessels by British artist Peter Layton.

Carved from soap, this contemporary version of a classical
ceramic vase is by the young South Korean artist Shin Meekyoung.

'Panier percé: le pot aux roses' is a do-it-yourself needlepoint-covered
bowl designed by French designers Guillaume Delvigne and Ionna Vautrin.
Image: Ilvio Gallo.

Traditional stamp and pot of red dye, Gahoe Museum, Seoul, South Korea.

Graffiti, often used for political message or gang
demarcation, finds a new life as alternative art form.

World War I experimental camouflage on warships,
designed to confuse submarine periscopes.

Above and overleaf — Banger racing liveries, painted for the last few hours
of the vehicles' lives, before the inevitable mutual mass destruction.

Pages 370 – 375 — Excessive ornamentation is often seen as poor design, poor taste or kitsch – but could equally be considered as good advertising, legitimate self-expression or entertainment.

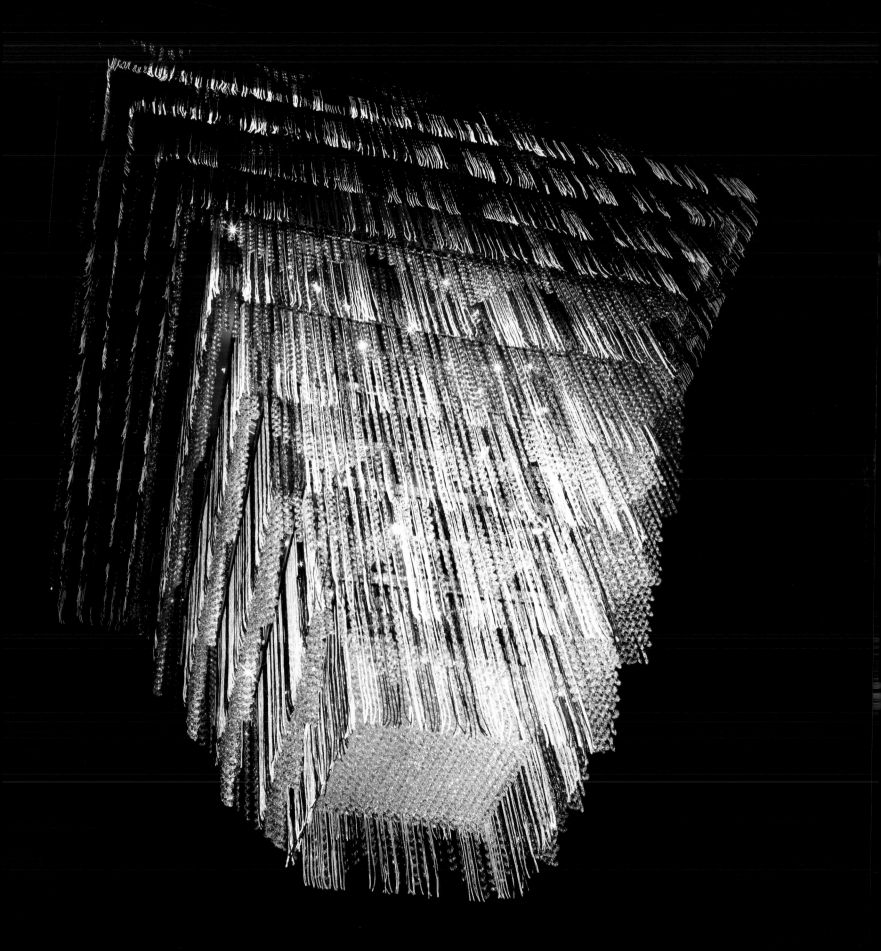

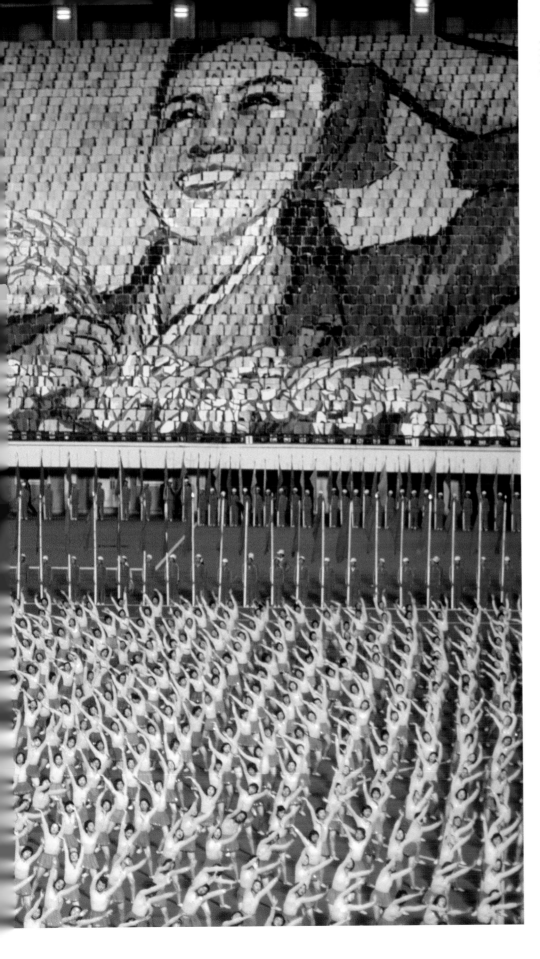

North Korean stadium imagery: individual coloured cards held up by thousands of audience members in synchronized unity create massive figurative illustrations.

Even seemingly functional textures are achieved using such materials as mesh, piercing, cobbling and non-slip flooring carefully arranged to please the eye.

Above and right — Irresistible opportunities to beautify
even the harshest man-made things: security fencing goes floral,
and iron railings get a comedy topping.

386 — 387 Expressionism

The most banal arrangements of basic building materials betray a
decorative interest in order.

Left, above and overleaf — Even the harshest living and working
environments reveal personalization and individual delineation of space.

The breadth and variety of colour preferences in low-cost
housing modules are here revealed on destruction.

Looking at the present state of industrial design, I see a visual language that is increasingly divorced from the functions and workings of the artefacts being designed. Take, for example, a vacuum cleaner, a cell phone, a suitcase and an automobile. These objects are now almost impossible to tell apart – their visual aspects are no longer related to their functions, and the materials and working mechanisms that previously would have defined their individual visual identities are no longer visible under the morphed skins of injection-moulded plastics.

In fact, it is now possible to make any object assume almost unlimited forms. This has come about partly through advances in moulding techniques in plastics and metals, and partly through a styling process. Reflecting the influence of the space age, it is akin to the streamlining craze that swept through the art deco and modernism periods from the 1920s to the 1950s. What is strange, though, is how limited a visual language has resulted from these unlimited possibilities.

More is less —
Another defining feature of our age is extreme choice, whereby the value of a tool is measured by its extra options. This is particularly obvious in the world of consumer electronics, in which artefacts that were previously controlled with one or two knobs (a radio or telephone, for example) are now host to a seemingly unlimited range of dials, switches and digital panels, rendering their complete functionality unlikely ever to be used.

Every day, in every way, life gets more complex, more detailed and more artificial. The amount of information, technology and change is increasing exponentially, so that it's extraordinary that we keep up at all. Sometimes one feels that with so many advances, and with progress occurring in so many fields, life should become simpler and functions should get easier – the modern life was supposed to be an absolutely seamless life… In reality, the exact opposite is true. I look at the tangle of wires, cables and small, mysterious plastic boxes next to my home computer and wonder how it has come to this. How can I regain an existence less dependent on complexity and artificiality?

I don't think that it's just me yearning for this – I can see it happening in all kinds of fields, including food, music and travel. It is a search for the real, the authentic, the gritty, honest and natural. In my own work and life, I find myself more and more attracted to the rough, the home-made, the uncomplicated and the individual or unique thing – whether that be in food, apparel or architecture – so I have called this *primitivism*, partly because it has a satisfying ring to it, but also because I believe that our headlong rush to modernity – our love and unstoppable adoption of the new – needs to be balanced by some human fundamentals belonging to earlier times.

Nature's gentleman —
Primitivism, the nostalgic belief that it is better to live simply, in a natural environment away from the constraints of urban society, was a popular

movement in philosophy and the arts during the eighteenth and nineteenth centuries. It held that people had lost touch with their roots and that civilized society lacked spontaneity, passion, mysticism and a closeness to nature. By contrast, the 'noble savage' living at one with nature in a pre-industrialized culture was believed to have an innate goodness and a sense of contentment.

But at the risk of appearing to wallow in a *nostalgie de la boue* (literally, 'nostalgia for the mud'– romanticizing the primitive), I feel that there is a lot to be learned from less 'developed' cultures. I am not suggesting that we should reject the modern world; on the contrary, I feel that a contemporary version is evolving. Thanks to the extraordinary potential of the information age, the rapid advancement of technology can be successfully married with the accumulated learning of the whole of humankind in a way that was never possible before.

Simplicity and sophistication —
You need only to look at a culture such as that of the Inuit, or Eskimos, to see that cultures described as primitive are, in fact, extremely sophisticated in many ways. They are, of course, far more in harmony with nature than we are. Their ability to survive in extreme climates using only local produce is extraordinary, as is their ability to craft high-performance transport, clothing and homes from the bare minimum of materials. No one looking at one of their kayaks can fail to marvel at the extreme elegance and economy of the construction and the beauty of the frame and hull. The garments crafted from animal skins perform in a superior way to synthetic modern equivalents, and the minimal beauty of an igloo is as stunning and innovative as any modern geodesic dome.

Another example is cooking. In many societies, a single small heat source and a small selection of implements provide the bare necessities to make a highly diverse and interesting menu. Think of the Moroccan charcoal stove with its earthenware tagine, or the Vietnamese noodle stall in the street serving delicious, inspirational and nutritious food for the whole community, using no more than a hot pot, some steam baskets and a wok.

In fact, a contemporary form of primitivism is happening in food. The commodification and processing of foodstuffs, which initially looked so modern and efficient, is now having all kinds of unforeseen consequences, and a counter-revolution is beginning. Today's consumer, sick of seeing identical apples in the supermarket, chicken breasts in clingfilm, and any amount of overpackaged convenience meals, has become angry and discerning and demanding. A new culture has emerged, as can be seen in the success of farmers' market, organic foods and the Slow Food movement. This new culture demands that food be fresh and untainted with chemicals, locally grown, and presented in a generous and unpretentious way in simple surroundings. No longer limited to high-end or middle-class restaurants, this approach is now commonplace. This is what's truly modern; the alternatives, such as overprocessed microwaved TV dinners, are looking increasingly passé.

Back to the drawing board —
So why can't the same attitude be seen as modern in the world of design? Isn't it time that the things around us felt real again, so that we can see the bits and pieces of functionality without everything being hidden inside a brightly coloured plastic case?

In the face of modern life's unparalleled complexity, it's only natural that a nostalgic view of the past should appear appealing. But whereas this approach was once retrograde and even dangerous, the significant difference today is that we are now in a position to pick and choose from an unlimited amount of information. We can assess and improve upon the lifestyles of a range of cultures and eras hitherto impossible to imagine.

High industrialization may well have provided us with an endless supply of cheap consumer goods, but the process has robbed us of much of the product personality and uniqueness that existed in the more local way of doing things. However, this is not a static state, and one result of the increasing uniformity in products and services is, paradoxically, the revival of the personal, the raw and the home-made.

Take bicycles, for example. The 'fixie' (fixed-wheel/fixed-gear bicycle) sub-culture that developed in New York with the adoption of track-bike technology among the city's bike couriers (see page 494) has become a world-wide phenomenon. With each bike being tailored by its owner into a dream machine, we have a mass-produced product being stripped down and customized to become a de-specced, simplified vehicle with the minimum of parts. Blogs on the subject disseminate information all over the world, parts are traded through Internet versions of the flea market such as eBay, and local manufacturers make small parts to customers' specifications using CNC (computer numerical control) programming and hi-tech numerically controlled machines. These activities are being replicated all over the world, where knowledge transfer and improved transportation links allow for a new individuality and self-reliance in producing things, where like-minded people can very quickly acquire and trade expertise and knowledge, and physical stuff. This points to a new future for designers, where they would be using their technical skills to seek out information about best practice from the whole massive Webbed world, gathering materials from an unprecedented global network and using the new technologies to provide customized, well-informed answers for all manner of local problems and opportunities. You might not get the fancy branding or the huge advertising campaigns any more, you possibly wouldn't get the absolute cheapest price, but you *will* get greater character, more local and personal solutions and a much happier customer who no longer feels like just part of the crowd, but instead has a car, house, pair of jeans or phone system completely matching his or her needs.

One of many hand axes that have been discovered at the
Homo neanderthalensis site of Swanscombe in Kent, England,
which was inhabited between 300,000 and 500,000 years ago.

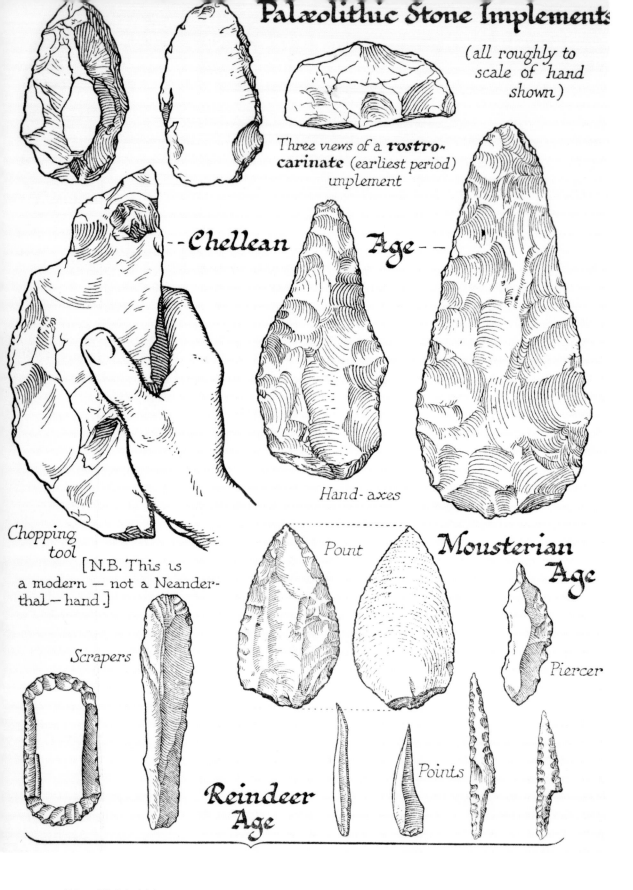

Palæolithic Stone Implements

(all roughly to scale of hand shown)

Three views of a **rostro-carinate** (earliest period) implement

Chellean — Age

Hand-axes

Chopping tool

[N.B. This is a modern — not a Neander-thal — hand.]

Point

Mousterian Age

Scrapers

Piercer

Reindeer Age

Points

Above and left — Early stone implements demonstrate
beauty, balance and function in a humbling display of design
skill from half a million years ago.

Cappadocian village of Ortahisar, Turkey,
an extraordinary integration into the landscape
that escapes most contemporary architecture.

Above and overleaf — Local materials create a design vernacular that
roots these cliff dwellings in the Gila Wilderness, New Mexico, USA.

Old domed mud houses in Kashan, Iran.

Traditional Yemeni houses in the Old City of Sana'a, Yemen. Several storeys high and topped with flat roofs, these tower houses are built of rammed earth and decorated with elaborate friezes.

Left and right — The headlong rush to colonize cities seems to have ignored all manner of alternative opportunities in living environments.

Above and right — Shanty dwellers demonstrate the
multiplicity of different approaches to building, completely
defined by availability of disparate material.

Above and left — An arctic igloo in the town of Churchill, in Manitoba, Canada, demonstrates economy of means and material to an extreme degree, epitomizing the human ability to innovate.

Steps are set into an old dry-stone wall on access land in the
Peak District National Park in Derbyshire, England – a design
detail mimicked by minimalist architects.

It took 2,000 years for the earthenware
Roman roof tile to be superseded.

Above and left — A round hut, with walls of logs, straw and mud, and a turf roof, in the Brithdir Mawr community near Newport in West Wales. The community is an example of a developing counter-materialistic movement that is taking the design and build of its environments back into its own hands.

Fishermen's park in Hellissandur, a village at the northwest tip of
the Snaefellsnes peninsula on the north coast of west Iceland.

Reconstructed traditional turf-roofed
building in Stokkseyri, southern Iceland.

A turf house dating from 1866 at Laufás Manor
Farm, near Akureyri, in northern Iceland.

Emma Orbach outside the round hut she built at the
eco-village of Brithdir Mawr, near Newport in Wales.

Modern technology and miniaturization will eventually allow the local individual once again to be designer and manufacturer in his or her own community.

Top row — In Delhi, Indian women use wooden blocks dipped in dye to print textiles. An Aboriginal man makes a bark painting in Arnhem Land, Northern Territory, Australia. David Magomwa makes sandals from old truck tyres; he has been making these sandals in a busy lane close to Kariakoo market in Dar es Salaam, Tanzania, for 25 years. A potter throws pots on a kick wheel in the village of Gunupur in the Indian state of Orissa.

Bottom left — Two workers print a Buddhist sutra at the Dege Scripture Printing Lamasery in Dege County, Sichuan Province, southwest China. The lamasery (a monstery for Tibetan Buddhist monks) owns more than 70 per cent of Tibet's sutraprinting blocks. Engraving printing is a traditional way to print the sutras. Workers write characters on thin papers and paste them face-down on the birch woodblocks, then engrave the reverse characters into the wood, cutting out the surroundings of the characters and leaving them elevated. After brushing the blocks with ink, they lay the paper on the block, then finish the printing.

The freshness and rawness of the produce in an Indian street
market seem refreshing to a supermarket shopper's jaded eye.

The role of product designers will have to evolve from one in which they are involved solely in the shape and function of the object, into one whereby they question all the factors involved in the artefact's creation and disposal. For this they will need to know about the sourcing and processing of the raw materials involved, the suitability and flexibility of the manufacturing process, the pricing and market research, the packaging, branding and promotion of the product, its distribution and – more and more pressing – its afterlife. The designer may even begin to question the very need for the existence of a new product, and it was this train of thought that led to the concept of Second Cycle. Initiated by the Finnish modernist furniture company Artek, the idea was born out of a love of the ageing process in the furniture that had come out of the factory decades earlier.

Artek is distinguished by the fact that it has made the same range of furniture, in the same factory, using the same birch wood from the same forest, since it was founded in 1935. Extremely hard-wearing, the furniture ages gracefully and is blessed with unusual longevity. As a result, revolutionary designs by the company's founder, Alvar Aalto, are available all over Finland, in various states of patina. Handed down over the generations, these vintage pieces of furniture reveal their history of use and misuse through the attractive layers they reveal.

In thinking about the nature of sustainability and questioning the validity of creating more stuff to fill the world with, Artek decided that it would be worth collecting some of these existing pieces and designing a system for putting them back into circulation. The exercise has begun with the stools, which are among the best-loved of Aalto's designs. The result is a strangely beautiful and gradually evolving collection in which the pieces are all the same yet all different, and curiously beautiful as their unique personalities evolve through an acquired personal history.

Original
ALVAR AALTO
design

2ND CYCLE
950 025

artek
made in Finland

Left, right and overleaf — Inspired by graffiti and children's art, the paintings of the French artist Jean Dubuffet (1901–85) compel the viewer to reinvestigate the world once it has been stripped of grown-ups' oversophistication.

456 — 457 Primitivism

An Aboriginal bark painting from Arnhem Land, in Australia's Northern Territory. One of the largest Aboriginal reserves in Australia, Arnhem Land is famous for its bark paintings, which are painted using earth pigments on interior strips of eucalyptus bark.

Left and right — 'Field', by British sculpture Antony Gormley, demonstrates the humanity, personality and uniqueness created through the simple gesture of squeezing a lump of clay and inserting two indents to form eyes. Where are the designers that demonstrate such personality in the mass-produced artefact?

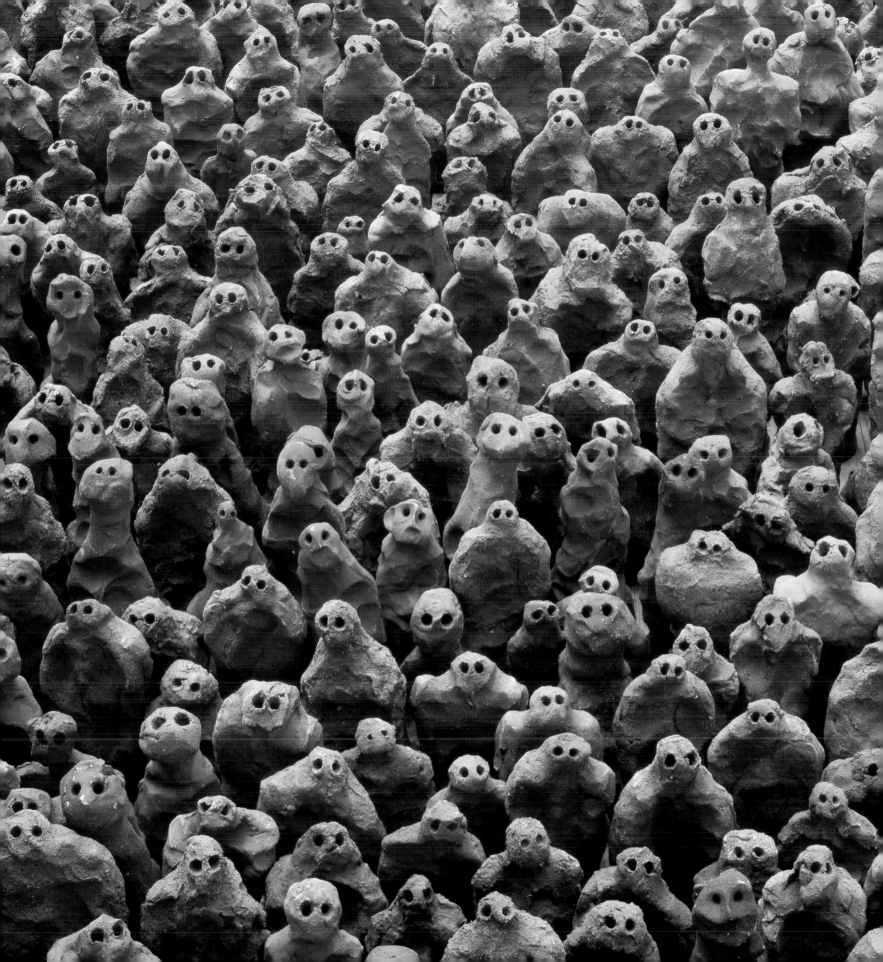

The rough and the under-designed are gaining momentum in an over-designed world.

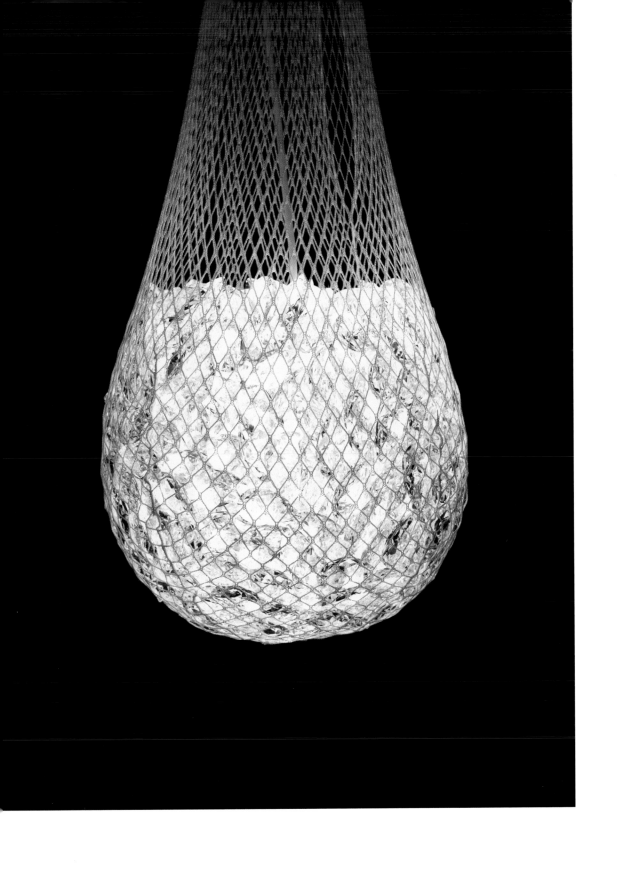

There is a primitive satisfaction that comes from
direct contact with the raw material of a product.

Left, right and overleaf — An in-built personality comes from the use of ready-made material. The raw, the untreated, the unfinished exude a material honesty absent from today's mass-produced consumer goods.

Left and right —
Loaded with history,
material quality,
texture and patina,
clear plastic refuse
washed up by the
sea makes up the 'Tide'
chandelier by the
London-based designer
and salvage pioneer
Stuart Haygarth.

Left, right and overleaf — Devoid of any extraneous decoration, here is design at its most basic.

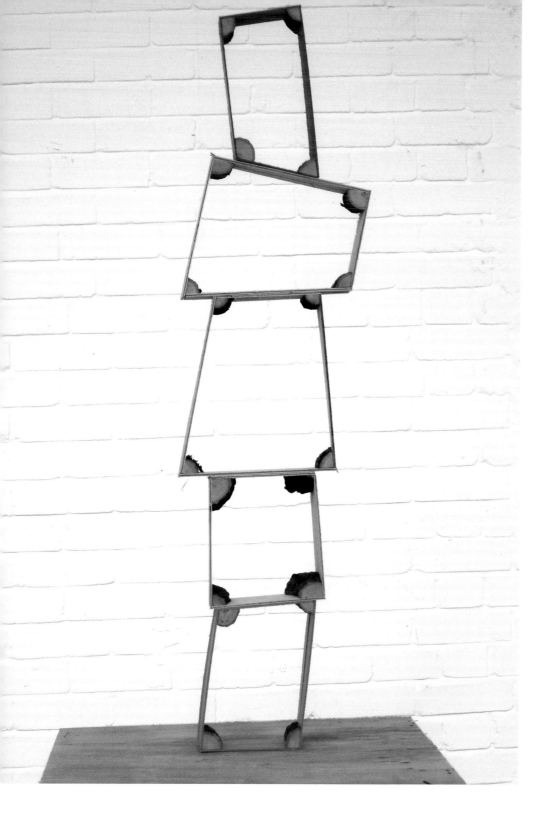

Watching television in a London
squat, an anti-design environment.

Above, left and overleaf — Scum City, by the Milan-based
product and furniture designer Jerszy Seymour, was a project where
a large amount of the design/construction process was left to
chance and installation-specific intervention.

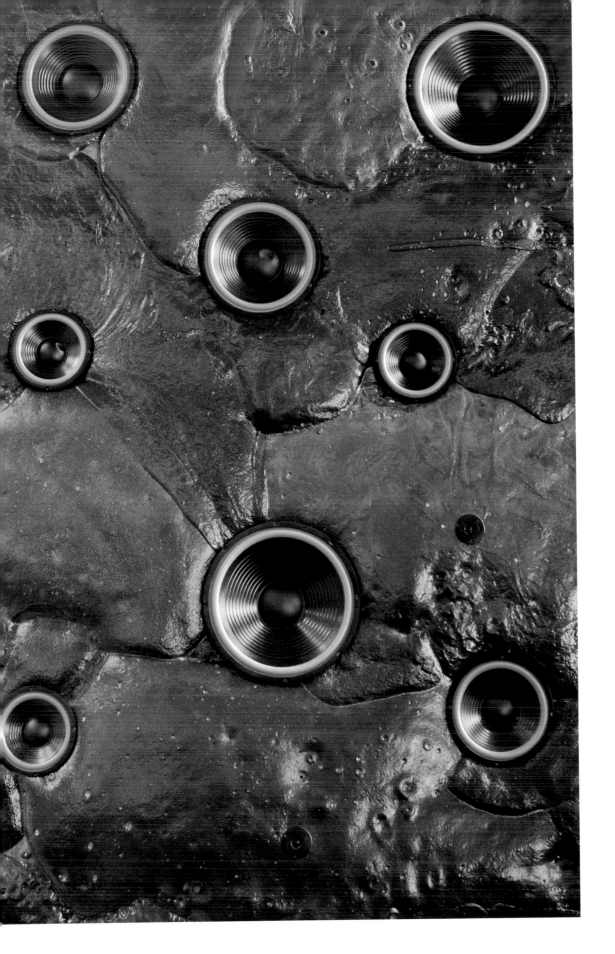

The headlong rush to consume that the world is involved in appears to be ever expanding. 'Gimme more, more, more,' we seem collectively to cry as we gorge ourselves on the remaining, increasingly limited resources that surround us. The constant warnings about the declining state of the natural world and the finite nature of its geological wealth are largely ignored.

Consumer goods galore —
Anyone who goes to a large trade fair in mainland China for, say, toys or gifts, cannot fail to be overwhelmed by the sheer, vertiginous scale of the mountain of goods now on offer. Equally, a visit to an export-focused factory in Vietnam or Taiwan makes all too clear the enormity of the effort to make us devour even more.

An unprecedented wealth of consumer goods threatens to bury us in an avalanche of truly grotesque proportions. The average British family has moved from owning 500 artefacts at the beginning of the 1900s to finding itself in possession of no less than 20,000 articles a century later. Encouraged by manufacturers, designers, retailers and marketeers everywhere, this unstoppable urge to consume is shored up by artificially cheap goods manufactured in vast volumes with little or no thought as to the long-term consequences. And I'm right there with the rest of them. Perhaps I'm even worse than most, as my job contributes to the problem – designing more stuff and then encouraging people to buy it is what I do. However, at the risk of sounding like a spoilsport, I feel that it may be time to look again at these patterns and try to define more mature ways of consuming.

Misgivings —
Maybe it was my own experience at Habitat that started me wondering about the nature of consumption and design. I spent six years assessing thousands upon thousands of designs, deliberating on their feasibility in production, arguing for their right to exist on the shop floor, estimating their potential for commerce, negotiating their buying price and, an even more laborious process, defining their colours and thinking of clever ways of launching them. This led me to a type of visual fatigue in which the merits of individual products faded in the general cacophony of new designs, new functions, new colours, new finishes.

Or perhaps it was the influence of my father, who quite rightly shuns any type of consumerism, finding it faintly obscene. He feels that in a world where so many people have so little, one should leave as small a footprint as humanly possible. Anyhow, whichever way you look at it, there is an increasingly strong case to be made for not engaging in extreme acquisition of stuff just for the sake of it.

Space invaders —
The modern dilemma as regards interiors and domestic environments, at least in the wealthy countries, is the war for space. The walls are effectively closing in

on us, for we are being overwhelmed by the expanding girth of our storage – the new shelves for our books and collections, the extra cupboards and closets for our shoes and souvenirs, the new hooks and racks for our bicycles and skis. Our floor space recedes as stacks of magazines and CDs and DVDs and video games mimic urban sprawl. Alongside these are tables and consoles to hold the ever-growing mounds of technology we now all seem to depend on: monitors, hard drives, processors and printers, with their accompanying tangle of cables that sprawl over the floors. Need I go on?

This nightmare vision is manageable only for the lucky few with large homes. The rest of us will have to find a new way of coping – a more enlightened way of consuming, a more judicious way of selecting the things we really need or cannot live without. In this hyper-consumerist age, how do we deal with the relentless pressure to acquire more? Can we possibly learn to collect carefully and be more selective? Can we even try to avoid having anything at all that is unnecessary?

To have or have not —
For early man, objects served only necessity, and stone tools for food and protection were crafted or acquired in a way that did not go beyond what was needed. Yet as historical record has proved, with society's increased wealth and sophistication comes a greater accumulation of things. Sometimes this has been linked to anxiety about less abundant times ahead, but often it has been the desire to impress – a visible show of status – or simply naked greed. Peer pressure is another factor, but the push to consume can come from the other end. As things become so widely available, cheap and cleverly marketed, and we become richer, the natural progression is to acquire and spend more. We do so without questioning whether the purchase is needed or even wanted – it is consumption as habit.

Yet this sequence has not always been inevitable. Historical examples abound of the rejection of worldly goods, although it is usually within a religious context. The Quakers have had their philosophy of 'plainness', the Taoists their emphasis on the absolute simplicity of living, the Buddhists their rejection of material wealth, and the monastic orders their pledge to sell all worldly possessions. This call for simplification seems even more appropriate in a contemporary context.

It's not just the material world that is overloaded. It is equally true of the 'software' that accompanies it – the relentless assault of sonic and visual stimuli which are so easy to access and so difficult to filter.

In this landscape it becomes increasingly valid to start thinking along reductionist lines. As I look at my own overloaded life, with the accumulation of things – the gifts that I would feel guilty about discarding, the holiday mementoes, the unused gadgets for cooking or cleaning – and the misguided

desire for more technology, I often wish that I had the courage to move out and leave everything behind. It would be like a reptile shedding his skin! How clean, pure and fresh I would feel to have nothing, and be able to start all over again. How much more discerning I would be in my new life – buying just what I need and no more. I would make educated and mature choices, and acquire only things of superior quality, which would last a lifetime or more.

Extreme simplification —
Reductionism extends far beyond a mere reaction to technological and consumerist overload. It is a necessary action to simplify and clarify our lives in an impossibly complex world. We are fortunate in having all of the tools at our disposal to lead simpler, enhanced lives. This may seem a tall order in a world where complexity is the rule, but there is better practice being demonstrated in many fields.

Take the example set by the bicycle couriers of New York. Here is a new business that has evolved from the dysfunction of contemporary life, in which the streets are clogged up by dirty, inflexible, over-engineered petrol-combustion vehicles, designed for five people but mostly carrying only one. As a result, the traffic grinds to a halt, forcing delivery companies with urgent post on their hands to choose the century-old human-powered bicycle as a modern tool for the fastest delivery.

A subculture has evolved in which the couriers compete over style and efficiency, using the latest advances in sports technology to strip down their cycles to the bare minimum. With hi-tech materials and highly engineered parts, they simplify their vehicles to the absolute maximum. Gone are the mudguards and the 32 gears. Even the back brake is seen as superfluous in the race to reduce the cycle to the bare essentials. The lessons here for designers are clear – even in a modern world, established technology can be reviewed, improved and put into service, and absolute simplicity can provide elegant solutions.

The redundant behemoth —
Another example, more anchored in technology, is the evolution of the music industry. Until very recently it depended on a massive infrastructure involving all the component parts of its creation and distribution. The recording took place in large studios with 64-track mixing desks and was followed by the cutting and pressing of vinyl in massive factories. The product was then distributed in large lorries and ships to warehouses worldwide, from which it was sent out to many disparate points of sale. There the discs would sit forlornly on shelves and racks waiting for a customer to notice them. The final stage of this complex and inefficient journey was to the consumer's home, where another object was added to the increasing clutter of the music lover's home.

In the new reductionist age, this whole chain of events has been completely displaced. Massive libraries of sounds and songs are now held in virtual form and added to by new talent who craft their tunes in garages and bedrooms or wherever else they wish. Using multipurpose compact tools (laptops to you and me), they access their consumers directly, without manufacturing or transporting anything physical. Their music is played on miniature devices a thousand times smaller than the radiogram or record player of two decades ago. Despite the evident lack of work for the product designer – no stereo systems, no record sleeves, no recording studio interiors or retail environments – the lesson is that the design of the *system* is the innovation.

The relevance and usefulness of design are enhanced by the application of design thinking to the entire chain of events, from the creation of the raw material to the consumption of the product. Although that may skip a series of product designs (much to the chagrin of record collectors), the result is an elegant solution for the musician and the audience, plus a massive saving in energy and artefact.

Efficiency and restraint —
Although this example is taken from another creative industry, it has important lessons that can be applied to any field. Inevitably, as the planet's population grows from its current 6.6 billion to an estimated 9 billion or more by the middle of the twenty-first century, clever design, engineering and technology will be needed. They will play an active role in encouraging moderation in material usage, restraint in systems of consumption and greater efficiency in everything we do. As it becomes increasingly clear how limited our natural resources are, we will all have to develop a reductionist attitude. Otherwise there will be trouble.

Despite the dream of a seamless, perfectly balanced life, most of us live in comparative chaos.

The number of possessions that we surround ourselves with is quickly spiralling out of control.

Left and right — The inner courtyard of the Gahoe Museum in Seoul, South Korea. Inspiration can be taken from other times and other cultures where less was needed and every possession fulfilled a specific purpose.

Left — Layered walk, typical of traditional Korean dwellings to protect the house, seen here in Samcheong-dong district of Seoul, South Korea.

Right and overleaf — The inner courtyard of the Gahoe Museum, Seoul.

Some societies have long adapted
to confined living spaces.

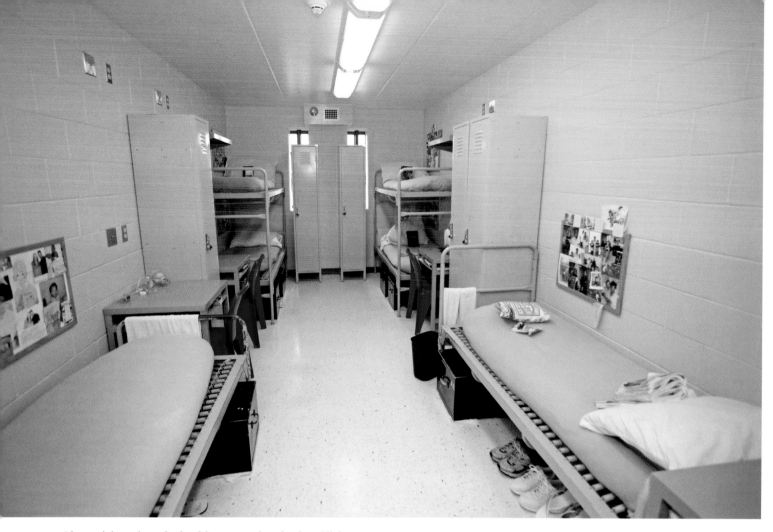

Above, right and overleaf — More examples of reduced living spaces,
by choice, by profession, by calling or through confinement, from barracks
to prisons to monasteries.

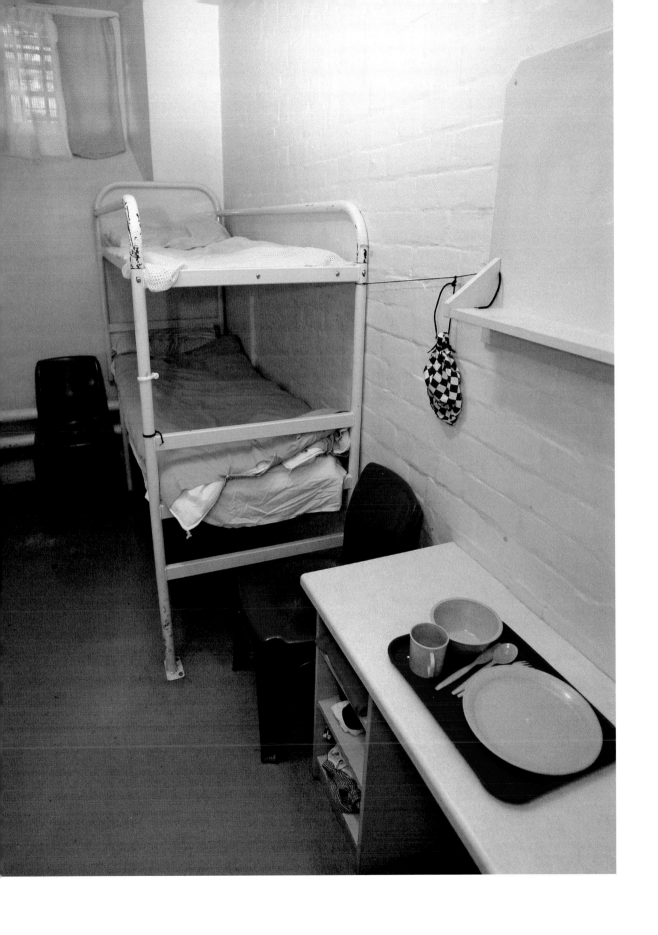

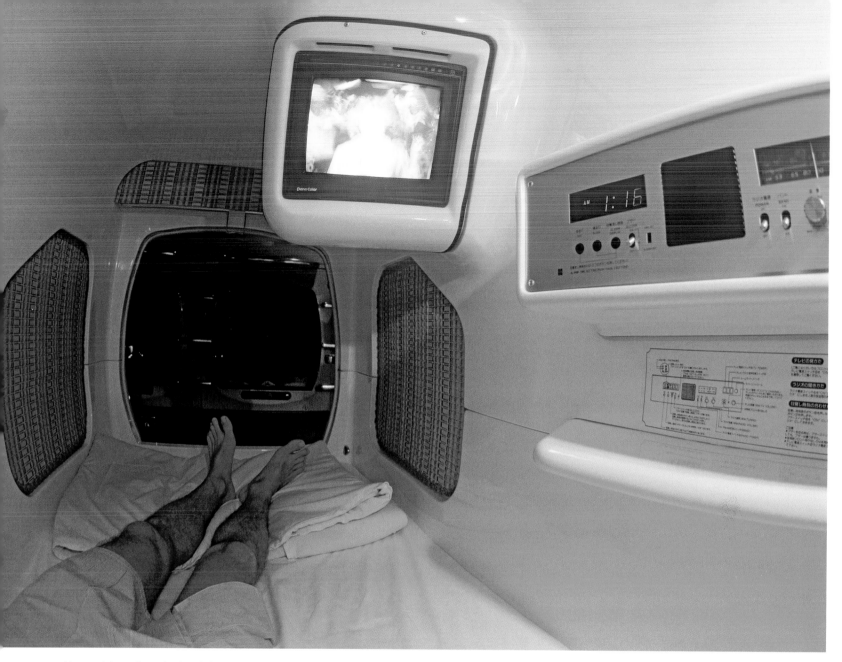

Above, right and overleaf — A Japanese capsule hotel redefines
the absolute minimum required for a specific activity. Having
tried one myself, I can report that this can work only for someone
of average oriental build, not a lanky westerner.

Traditional hut of the San people in Kuboes town in the Richtersveld,
South Africa. The landmark Rhenish church dates from 1893.

Above, left and overleaf — An avant-garde project by the German industrial design guru Luigi Colani and Hanse Haus in 2004, the Rotor House offers the ultimate in compact living. A living room surrounds a central core containing the functional areas of kitchen, bath and bed, which, thanks to a remote-controlled rotor, can be rotated to give access to the required space. As a result, a space only 6m (20ft) square provides actual living space that feels much larger.

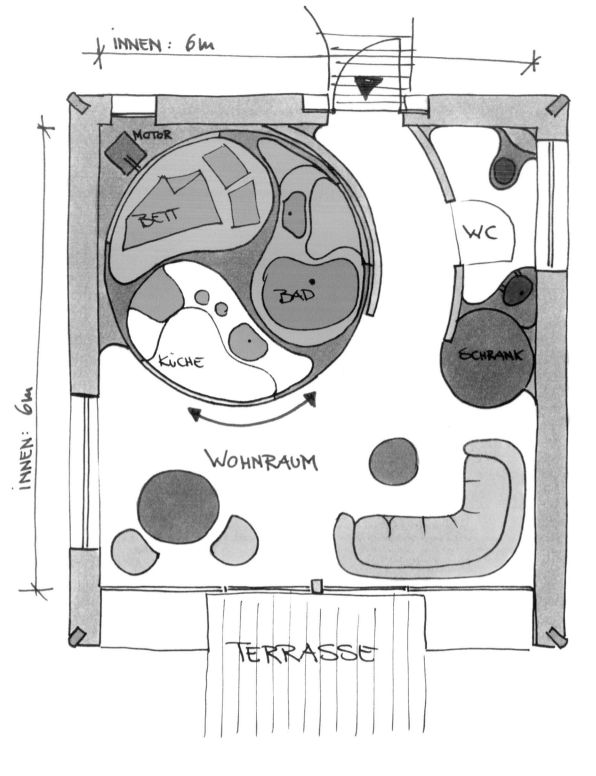

INNEN: 6m

INNEN: 6m

MOTOR

BETT

BAD

Küche

WC

SCHRANK

WOHNRAUM

TERRASSE

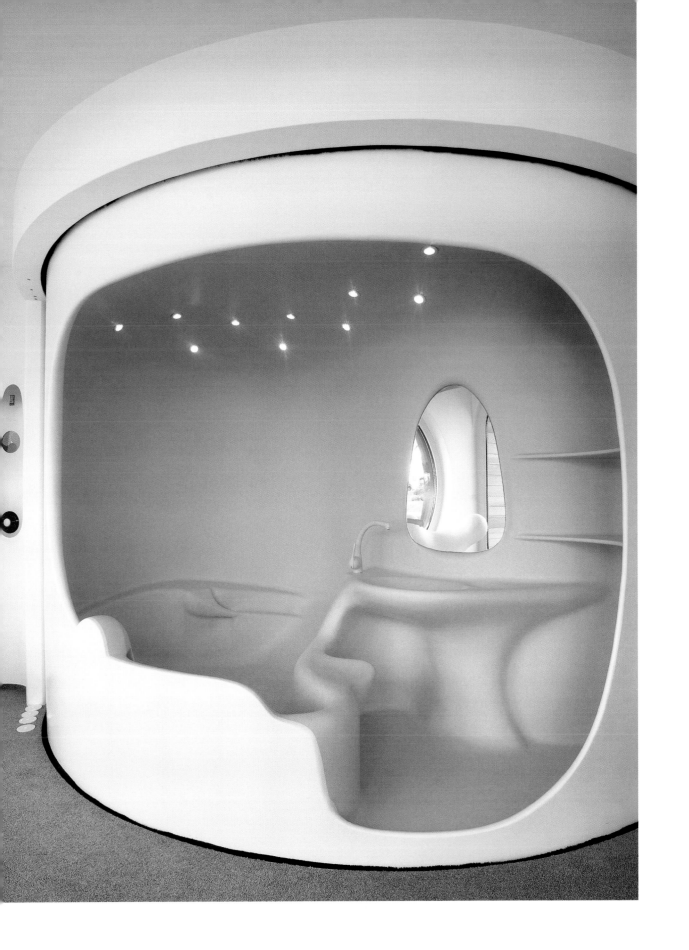

Above and overleaf — Constructed from repurposed drainpipes,
dasparkhotel is a hostel set in a park near the Danube in Linz, Austria.
It was conceived and implemented primarily as a hospitality tool, and
each drainpipe contains a double bed, storage, lighting and power.
Guests, who are asked to pay what they can, share bathroom facilities.

Above and right — The micro compact home, or m-ch, is
a lightweight compact dwelling for one or two people which is
available throughout Europe. A 2.6m (8.5ft) cube, it can be
adapted to a variety of sites and circumstances. Its functioning
spaces of sleeping, working/dining, cooking and hygiene
make it suitable for everyday use on a short-stay basis.

Above and left — Container City is a versatile modular system that provides funky, cheap and flexible accommodation for a range of uses. Devised by Urban Space Management, the system uses shipping containers linked together to provide strong, prefabricated steel modules that can be combined to create a range of building shapes. If desired, they can be clad in a variety of materials. When no longer needed on a particular site, they can be unbolted and either relocated or stored.

Above and right — Appropriately for a company that makes bags from recycled materials (bike inner tubes, car seatbelts and truck tarpaulins), the Freitag shop on a freeway in Zurich, Switzerland, is made from 17 rusty, recycled shipping containers. The 26m (85ft) high concept store illustrates the reduction of design input to a selection of a set of ready-mades.

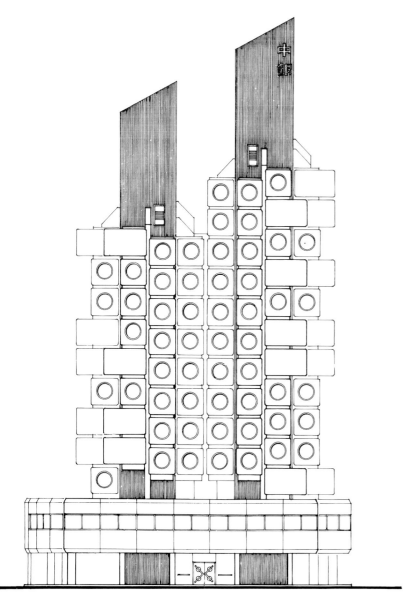

Above, right and overleaf — Completed in 1972, the 13-storey Nakagin Capsule Tower in Tokyo was the world's first example of capsule architecture built for actual use. The architect, Kisho Kurokawa, developed the technology to install each of the capsules into a concrete core with only four high-tension bolts, as well as making the units detachable and replaceable. A capsule, which measures 2.3 x 3.8 x 2.1m (7.5 x 12.5 x 7ft), functions as a self-contained small living space or office, but capsules can be combined. Complete with appliances and furniture, from audio system to telephone, each capsule was pre-assembled in a factory, and was then hoisted into position by crane and fastened to the concrete core shaft.

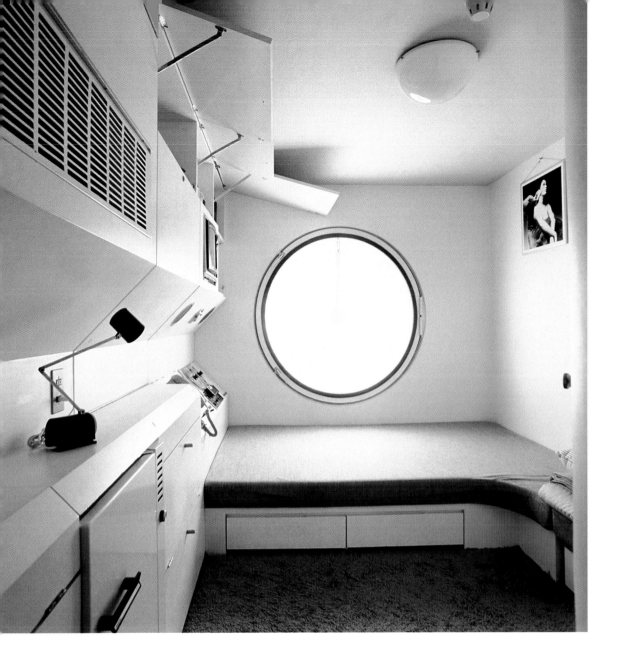

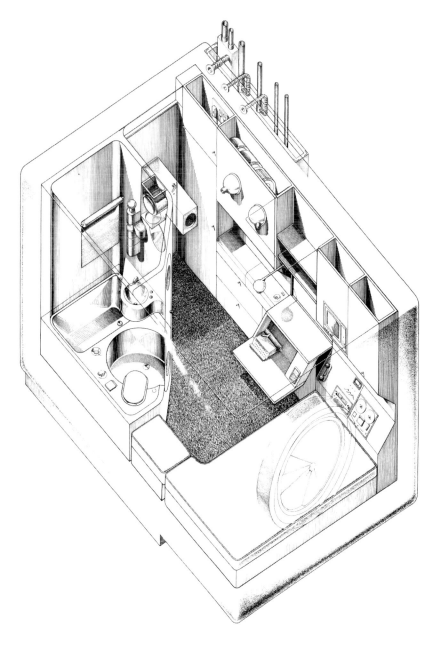

Inside easyHotel, the idea that customers will accept
less space for a better price.

The British design collective Inflate's
temporary office in London.

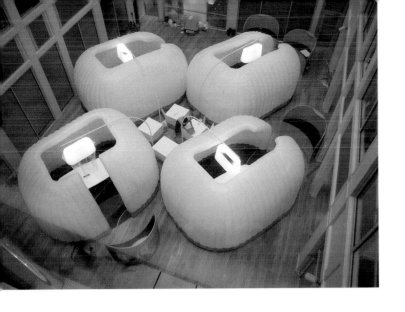

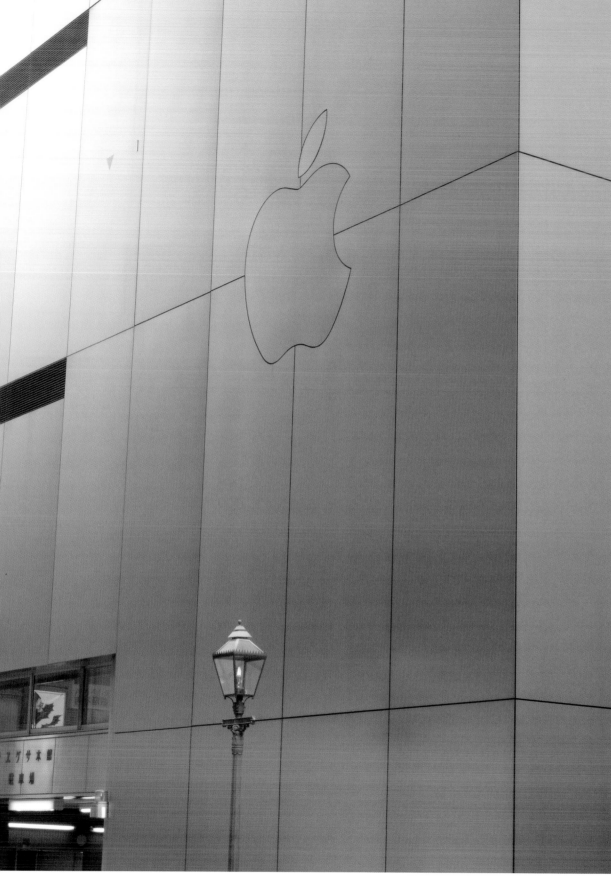

Left — Neo-brutalism in an Apple store.

Right — Original brutalism in London's National Theatre, designed in 1976–7 by Sir Denys Lasdun.

This stripped-down, material-heavy style of architecture is only just beginning to re-emerge.

Left, right and overleaf —
Architectural elements with
a design language devoid of
anything but pure structure.

The bare minimum —

Reductionism is found in many fields, from cuisine to architecture. However, it is particularly compelling in the extreme world of minimal and conceptual art, where the challenge to notions of consumerism can be taken to its radical conclusion.

This is nowhere better expressed than in the work of Michael Landy, one of the so-called Young British Artists. Over a period of two weeks in 2001, in an exhibition called *Break Down* that he held in an empty department store in London's Oxford Street, Landy proceeded to catalogue and then destroy every single possession that he owned. The detailed, computer-printed inventory, which was hung on one wall of the installation, itemised more than 7,000 objects, ranging from his David Bowie records, his private letters and his father's sheepskin coat to original artworks, electrical equipment and his Saab car. All were shredded and pulverized by Landy and his ten assistants using industrial machinery. Landy pronounced himself liberated through dispossession, although side effects did take place (such as the loss of a desire to produce new work, and the inability to travel abroad owing to the lack of a passport). Through questioning the need for artefacts, Landy demonstrated the opportunity available to all of us to divest ourselves of possessions and lead a simpler, freer existence.

Further inspiration is to be found in the sculptures and installations of the British artist Martin Creed. Creed's examinations of the minimal are inspirational through their re-contextualizing of everyday elements in a way that focuses on their very banality: a stack of plywood, a light bulb switching on and off. If only we could look at and appreciate the simplicity of everyday objects in this rigorous way, our perception of life might be expanded and enhanced.

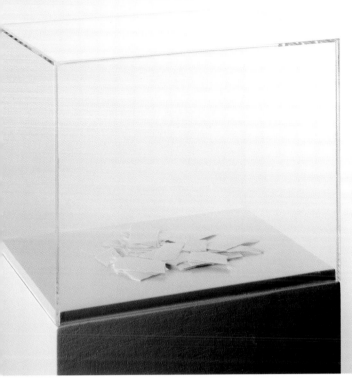
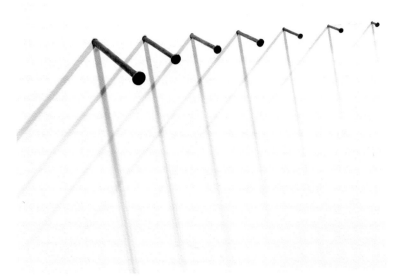

The 'Break Down' project.

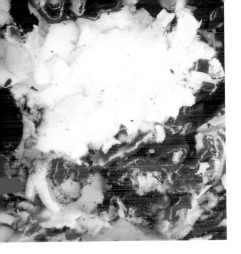

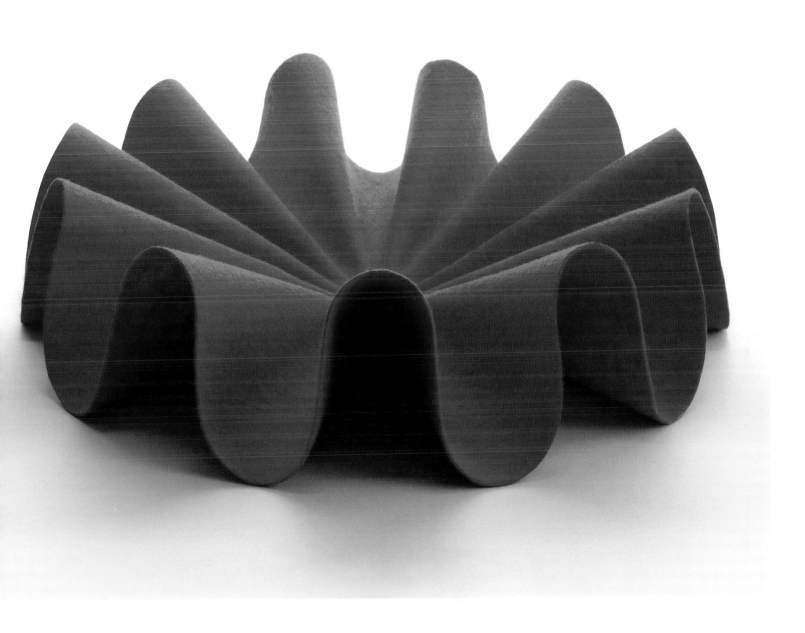

HONEYCOMBLAMP

made in Japan

from Kyouei Co.,Ltd

Above and left — The Honeycomb Lamp by the Japanese company Kyouei Design is made from denguri paper, a product of Japan's Shikoku region. The lampshade, which is only 2cm (¾in) thick when folded flat, is shaped like a lamp. After it is unfolded, wrapped around a light bulb and pinned in place, it creates a lantern-like effect.

Above and left — Pure structure as a decorative element.

Above and right — Some basic needs.

Lao Buddhist monks on their morning
rounds of begging for alms for sustenance.

Buddhist monks eating at Kya Khat Waing
monastery in Bago, Burma (Myanmar).

Lesotho, 2004: a man with his radio
powered by a broken piece of solar panel.

A solar cooker in India.

Not so long ago it was commonplace for magazines, newspapers and television shows to present a bold and often completely fantastical vision of the future. We were promised so much, from personal planes and domestic vacuum-cleaning robots to mobile living pods and home dry-cleaning. Earlier still, in the 1950s and '60s, wipe-clean, brightly lit space-age interiors were temptingly envisioned where domestic chores were a thing of the past. Acres of spotless, neon-lit, patterned Formica allowed for total hygiene, and even food preparation was reduced to a scientific laboratory process.

Underlying this sort of vision was an unswerving faith in the power of technology to create a better quality of life, and an ever-present optimism about how progress could benefit human beings. A lot of the visions we have today are about further leaps forward in technology. For sure, some of it will come true; however, like science fiction's spaceships that were riveted together in a completely improbable way, these things can be based only on the technology available at the time and the limitations of the imagination.

You'd think that by now we might have been getting better at predicting the course of innovation. However, the only thing that is clear at the moment is that the pace at which things are changing makes the development of our future even more unpredictable than it was. You can't anticipate what people will be able to do in the future. The only given is the speed at which it happens.

What is also apparent now is that the optimistic predictions of yesterday have been replaced with a more apocalyptic vision of the future. The statement that this is the first generation that believes it doesn't get any better, and won't get better for their children either, is now widely quoted. It's a chilling thought that until now people were optimistic about the future, thinking it couldn't get any *worse* – it's as though we have somehow peaked.

From looking at interior design magazines now, it would appear that the vision of the future lies in ever more dispiriting ways to tackle storage in constrained spaces as our families fragment and house prices soar. Our increased ability to buy cheap goods allows us to fill these shrinking homes with more stuff that we were not even sure we wanted and didn't even realize we needed until last week.

As our future existence unfolds, we flick through the pages of the gossip rags and gaze at the *'lives of the rich and famous'* television shows that flaunt the implausibly opulent and spacious pads of the super-rich. How sad to witness the inevitable addiction to the neoclassical, the overblown chandeliers, the monogrammed sheets and cream carpets from the very people worshipped because they are the latest pop sensations, the most creative IT specialists or the most gifted sportspeople.

It would be easy to believe that all things are bleak in the interior world, but in reality the future has already arrived, and we live with it every day.

One big problem with foreseeing the future is that it is now becoming increasingly invisible. Allow me to explain. How do we make the centrepiece of our home the radiogram when it has shrunk to fit into the palm of our hand? What has happened to the mighty kitchen range, which from being the very heart of the home has quickly declined? First it became a compact fitted cooker built into the kitchen surface, then it further shrank as it mutated into the miserably minute microwave, declining even to have a space-age housing and retaining all the personality of a transistor radio.

The focus of our lives in the past few decades has rapidly transferred from sofa and television to a fragmented series of work/entertainment consoles, where individual members of a family pursue solitary pleasures in the virtual auction houses, gambling dens or social clubs that used to be such real physical spaces. No longer is the dining table a fixed meeting point, as different dietary requirements, fragmented eating patterns and snacking in front of television replace the venerable, social, three-course dinner, and breakfast is reduced to a double skinny latte on the march from bus stop to work.

From a situation 60 years ago where people huddled around a radiogram listening to, at best, three or four radio stations, we moved rapidly to a scenario 20 years later where the family gathered on the sofa gazing at a single television in regular programmed viewing patterns. How different from today, as the family fragments to watch YouTube downloads on hand-held devices or scatters around the house to send emails. And this is clearly just the beginning.

In truth, the focus of our living arrangements is in a process of constant and revolutionary change for which there is little possibility of finding a visual language. This is partly because of the speed at which technology and ways of living currently mutate, but also because of the way that change is happening, both in manufactured objects and, especially, in the digital world. A very visible example is the evolution of sound and the moving image in the home.

What is happening at the moment is that we're layering innovation over innovation, and creating a totally confusing landscape. One has to hope that in the future it will be seamless and that things will be much more human-orientated.

Most people are living now in a state of total cabling overload, and it is completely beyond their ability to control it. Think how thick the manuals are for your mobile phone, or what you could do with your video recorder that you'll never discover, or the power needed for computer applications you'll never use. We have become quite phobic about technology, hoping for the development of interfaces that are more intuitive. But what inevitably happens is that things become rapidly redundant as they don't succeed and other things are improved.

A rapid type of natural selection is occurring in technology, and the impact it has on our environment and how we arrange the objects around us means that we are constantly being tested as to which direction to take. We are in limbo between the old and the new, and we have to be conscious that the technology available to us is merely a set of tools that can be used in any way. As with the splitting of the atom, domestic technology can be used for peaceful means or for the most abominable destruction.

There is, however, hope. The beauty of the new tools at our disposal is that they are personal. You can print your own book these days, and creating your own furnishings is easy now. However, people have not yet caught on to that, so we will see things changing very rapidly as time unfolds. We must realize that there are potentially a vast number of positives within technology, but it's down to people to determine whether it's going to dehumanize interaction or our personal sense of self. The choices are open to us right now.

The next few years will surely bring the blending of wall and screen to the point where we no longer need light fixtures, televisions or computer units as artefacts. They will start to blend into the architecture of walls and ceilings as light-emitting wallpapers. Devices that previously demanded furniture to sit on while they were being used (telephones, radios, computers, televisions) will become so miniaturized that they will slip into your pocket.

The buildings themselves will increasingly be able to respond to our needs, as a type of ambient intelligence will allow the systems we install to adapt to our preferences. We will be the inhabitants of 'living' systems rather than of static buildings. These dynamic structures will even modify their internal and external forms in response to changes in their environments. Houses might expand and contract to reduce surface area and cut heating costs in the winter, and they could cover themselves to escape the heat of the summer sun.

The potential that is emerging in terms of sheer computing power, miniaturization and nanotechnology is just phenomenal. As regards communication, individuals can now become virtual groups all around the world, sharing problems. The information is instantly disseminated, allowing people to gain knowledge in record time through the new media. The personalization of technology that used to be available only to major companies and big industries is now becoming accessible to all, and the implications are only just starting to reveal themselves.

In the meantime, though, the radical developments in manufacturing technology are, after many false starts and over-optimistic promises, finally upon us. The constraints inherent in the previous, old-fashioned manufacturing techniques are now set to vanish, as computer-controlled machines allow every design fantasy to become real. As already mentioned, this could bring extraordinary liberation to the designer, but is equally a recipe for unlimited amounts of rubbish. The dreams of science-fiction interiors are now realizable. At the cutting edge, a design aesthetic is evolving that will inevitably implode on itself as designers use increasingly sophisticated numeric modelling techniques to outcurve each other in a direct challenge to the feasibility of current manufacturing techniques, making buildings and objects that are purely an experiment in the audacious, or the never-been-done, rather than a service to people and their needs. So we are still very much in an interim state of being, where the design tools being put at our disposal are way in advance of the means of production.

The 'houses of the future' that were dreamed up in the 1960s were developed against the backdrop of the space race, but today the question is whether our unchecked technological evolution is going to help or hinder life in the future. Design was expected to ease the lives of the inhabitants of the twenty-first century, but, through the creation of more and more gadgets and gizmos, it often seems just an instrument to facilitate extreme consumption, increased complexity and ever-increasing pace, thanks to 24-hour communication, faster transport and global competition.

An alternative is fast developing, though, that could just save us from this nightmarish vision. 'Micro' seems now to be plausible as an alternative. Small is beautiful again, but this time it doesn't necessarily have to be low-tech. Micro-generation of power, local manufacturing, local production, local water purification – all are possible now, even to the point of their being done by small communities or the individual. All of this will have an impact on the built environment generally. Running your life eventually to achieve zero-energy living, then going beyond and feeding something back into the grid will become the goal, allowing people to take control of their environment.

Technology can be harnessed to contribute to a greater, more global cause. With so much fear and confusion around at the moment, it is easy to lapse into pessi-mism but, on closer inspection, the tools to change are rapidly emerging and will be put at our disposal.

Future cycle. Designer Mr B. G. Bowden
with his new 'electric bicycle', which he
is taking to the offices of the Council of
Industrial Design, for inclusion in the
Britain Can Make It Better exhibition of
1947. It had a dynamo that stored energy
while travelling downhill and released
it on upgrades – design as a motor for a
competitive edge.

The future of commuting, *circa* 1958: a futuristic monorail for the year 2000
to transport people to and from suburbia and to their waiting families. If only!

Los Angeles International Airport's landmark
Theme Building, which opened in 1961.

Audiovisual headset that replicates the experience of
viewing a 132cm (52in) TV screen from 2m (6ft 6in) away.

An ultra-modern globe stereo system designed by David Sykes
of London is demonstrated at the Here Tomorrow exhibition in 1970.

A revolving kitchen which won first prize in the
Bird's Eye design award 1968 for Ilana Henderson,
a student at London's Royal College of Art.

Revolutionary spheroid plastic houses at the 'world's first international
plastic housing exhibition' held in Lüdenscheid, Germany, in 1971. Plastic
is one architectural material that stubbornly refuses to arrive, despite
advances in building technology.

An architect's model of 'Skyport 2000', a futuristic 1957 proposal for an airport building to stand in St George's Circus, near Waterloo Station, London, in the year 2000. Made for the Glass Age Development Committee and designed by architect James Dartford, the model shows how aircraft could land and take off from a giant platform supported by three glass-clad pillars. These would contain elevators carrying passengers down to a hotel, offices and parking for private planes and cars.

Visitors to the 1939 New York World's Fair (theme: 'the World of Tomorrow') entering the
Perisphere, 55m (180ft) in diameter, which contained a diorama depicting a city of the future.

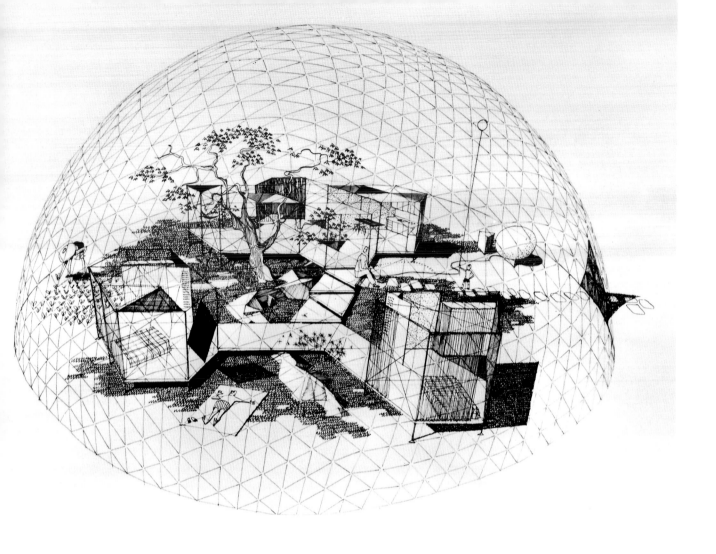

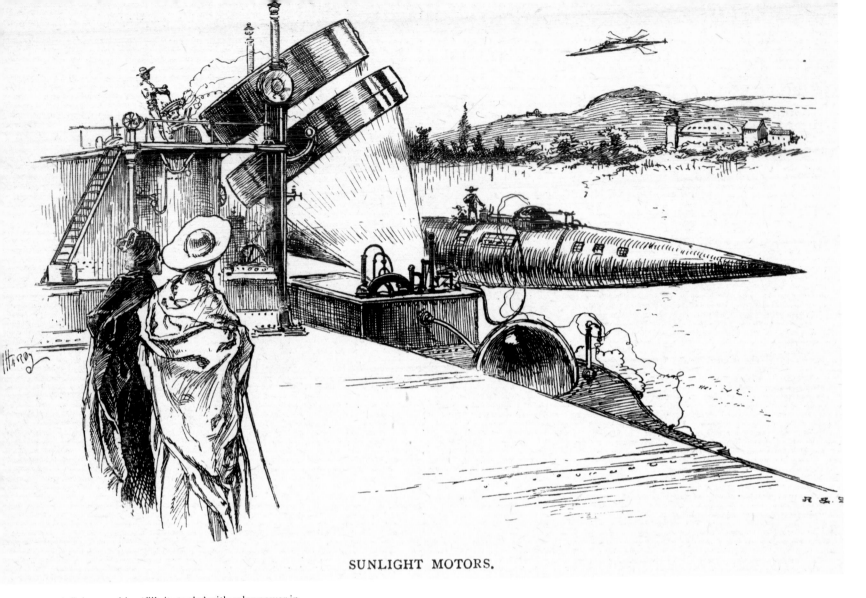

SUNLIGHT MOTORS.

A flying machine 'fills its tanks' with solar power in
an illustration by Paul Hardy in *Cassell's Magazine*, 1898.

24-FOOT SPACE STATION
FULL SIZE TEST MODEL

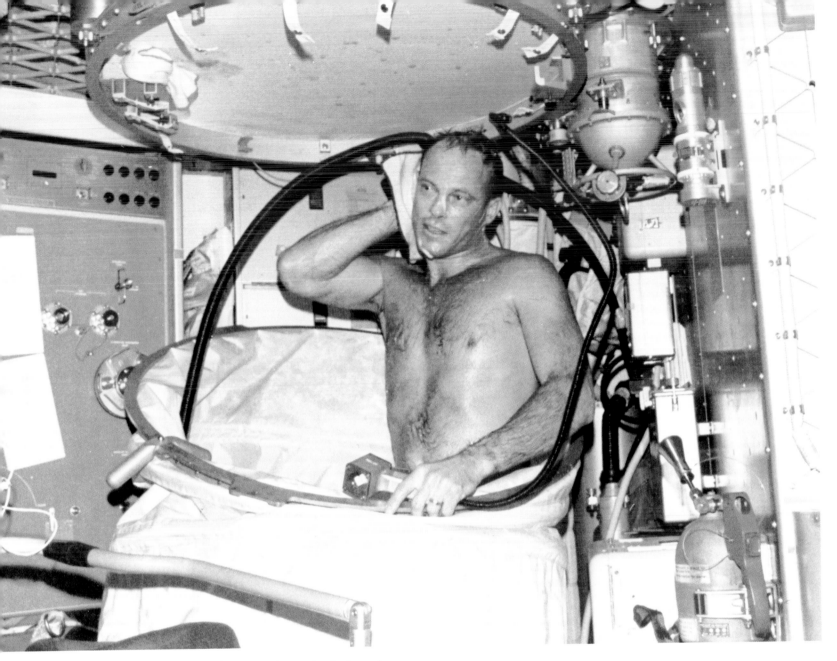

Above and right — The realities of space travel prove harder to crack,
and present many complexities in mundane everyday activities.

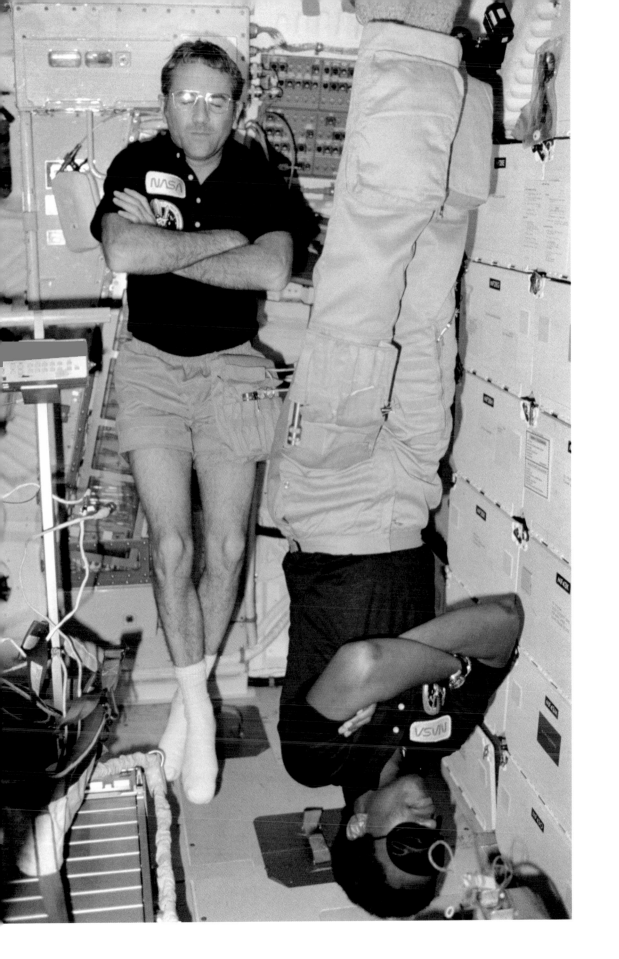

Above and right — Vast, self-sustaining space colonies providing
artificial gravity no longer seem so possible or even desirable.
Maintaining and repairing the damage done back home would
seem a more urgent priority.

The phallic 1970 sports car, the C11, is an iconic example of German designer Luigi Colani's thrusting biomorphic design genius.

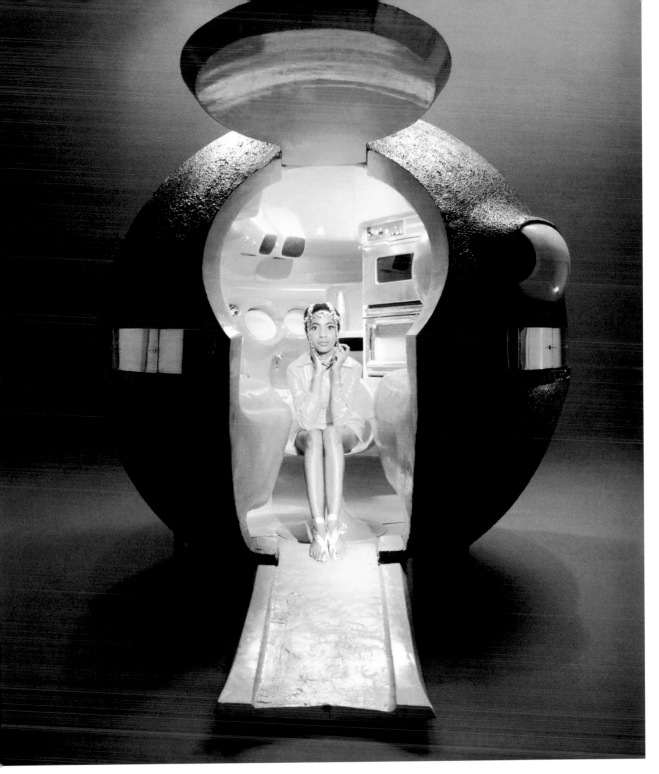

Designed by Luigi Colani for Poggenpohl of Germany in 1968/1971, this spherical kitchen was designed to hang like a satellite from an elliptically shaped residential module.

This 1973 Luigi Colani study of a possible shape for
a motorcycle was based on studies of frogs.

The Museu de Arte Contemporânea in Niterói, Brazil, was designed by
the futurist Brazilian architect Oscar Niemeyer, who defined the optimistic
futuristic architecture of the 1950 and 1960s.

The Palm Project, an artificial island off the shore of Dubai. Built in the shape of a palm tree, it epitomizes the hopeless kitsch of current developments.

An oil refinery is a more realistic symbol of the shape of the future.

Above and right — An inflatable bridge is a more
temporary and flexible form of architecture.

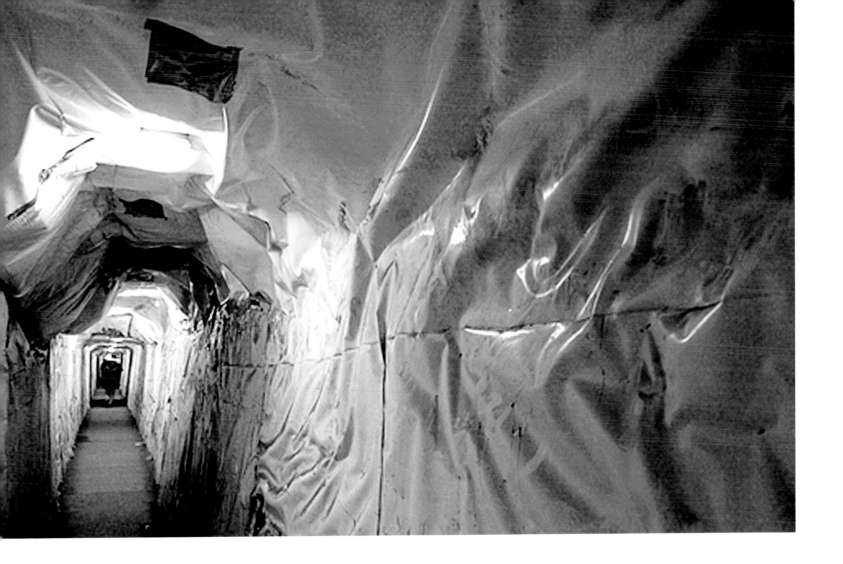

Above and right — Futuristic architecture, easily dreamed up by computer-propelled designers, is often still laboriously hand-built using craft skills.

Above and right — Construction techniques are slowly catching up with innovative designers' demands.

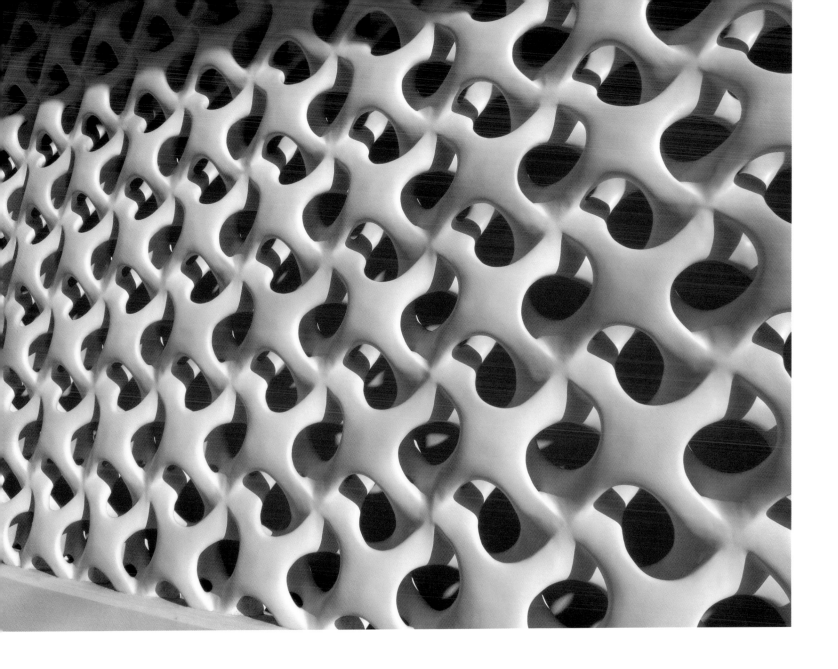

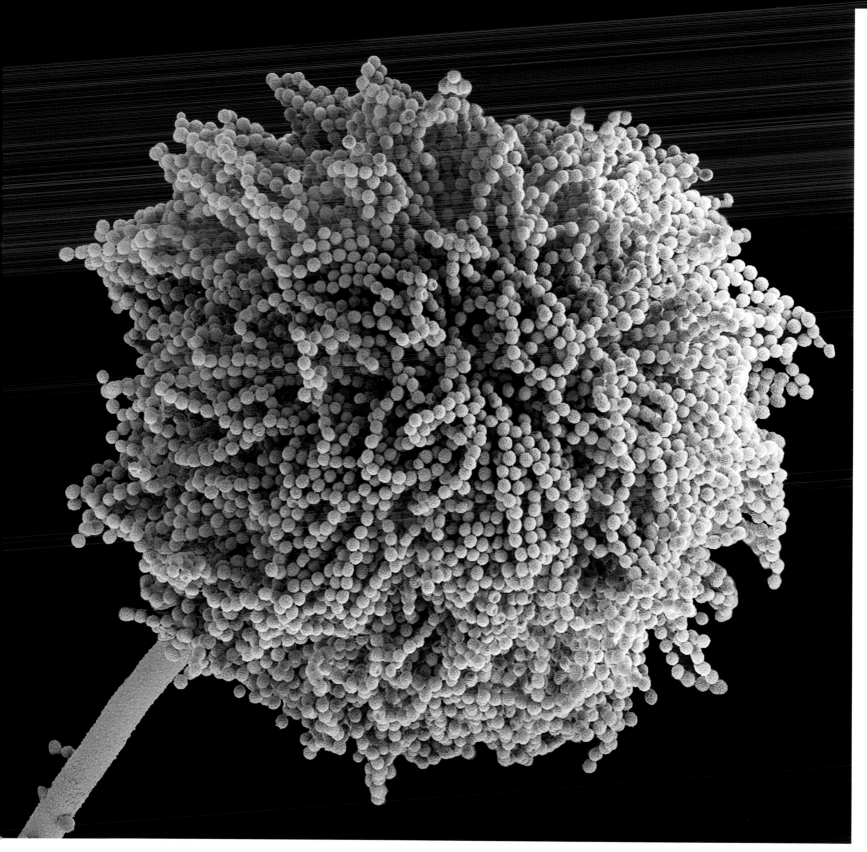

Increasingly the lessons learned from biology and chemistry will allow designers to mimic the economy and elegance of nature. This coloured scanning electron micrograph (SEM) shows fungal spores (reproductive cells) on a fruiting body of an *Aspergillus* fungus, which mostly grows on decomposing organic matter. The fruiting body, or conidiophore, consists of chains of numerous small spores that are dispersed by the wind to form a new fungal body.

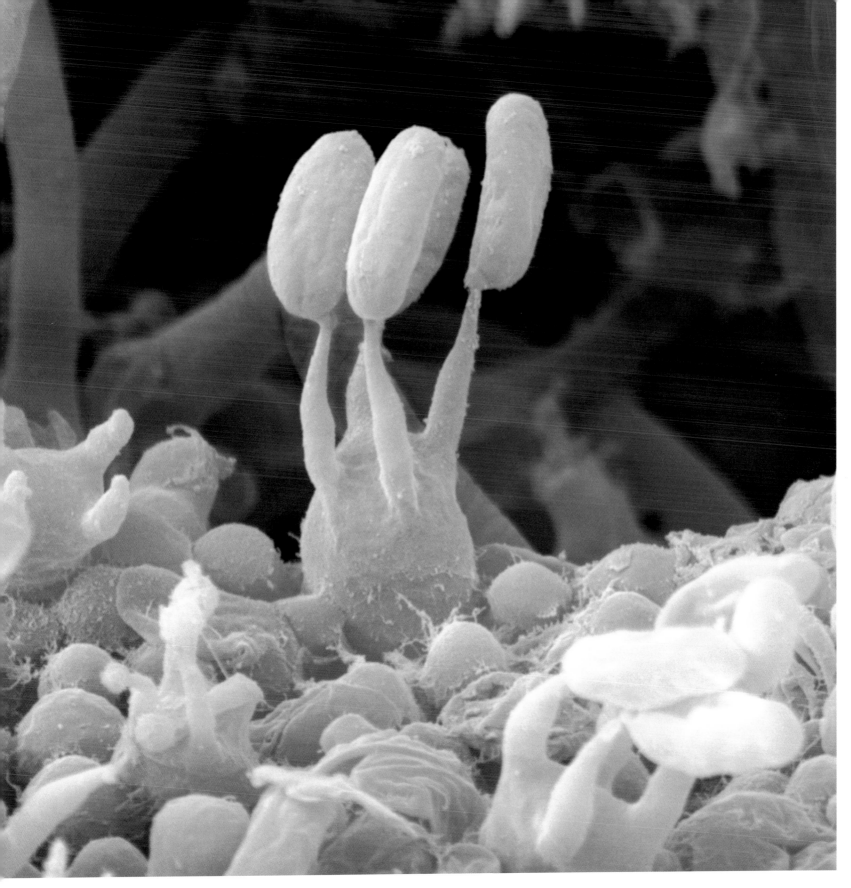

Above and overleaf — Fungal spores.

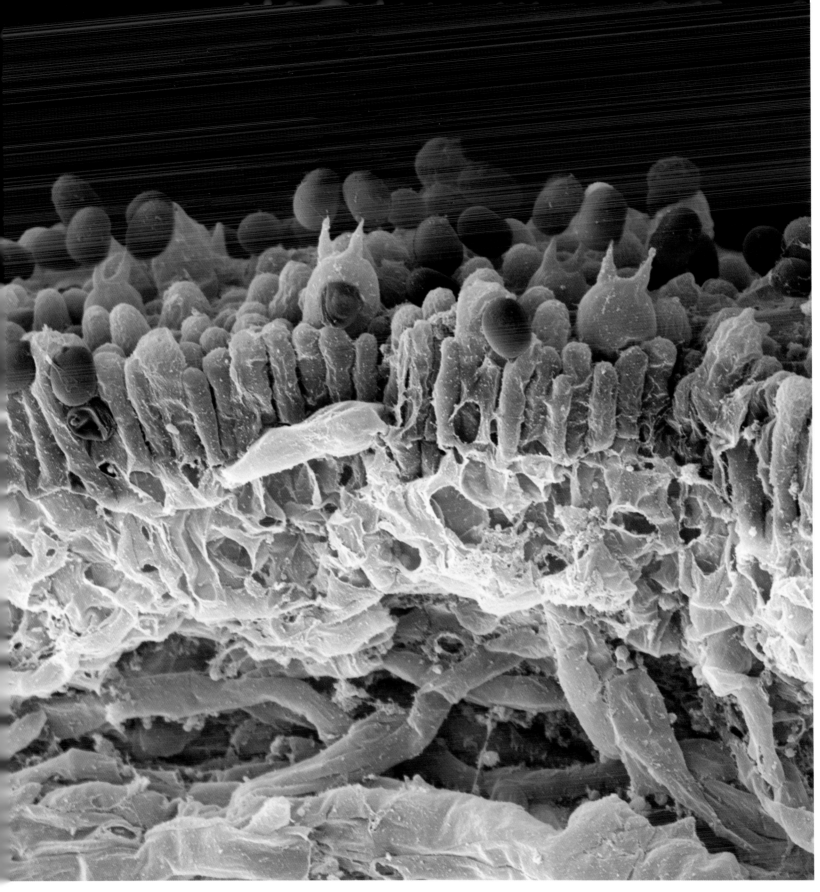

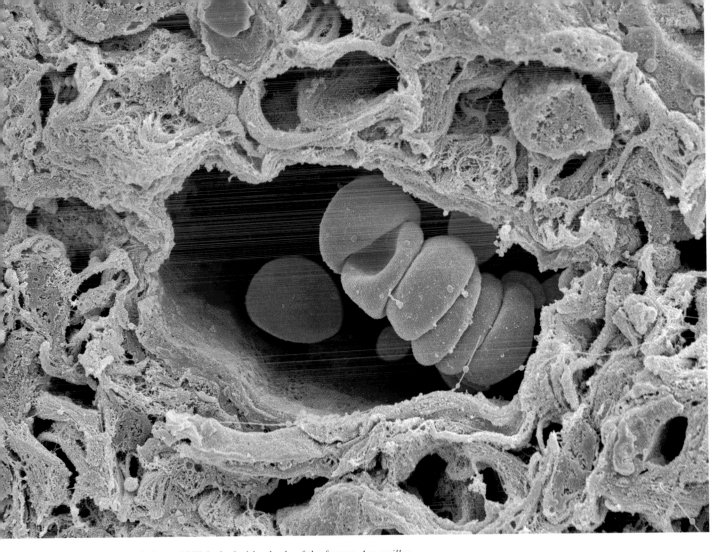

Previous page — Coloured SEM of a fruiting body of the fungus *Aspergillus niger*. The small, white, spiky spheres are spores, which are about to be released into the air. This fungus grows in household dust, soil, and decaying vegetable matter, including stale food.

Above — Coloured SEM of a cross-section through a small thin-walled artery known as an 'arteriole'. Red blood cells are seen in the central space. Understanding the growth and structure of living bodies is increasingly informing the construction and design of the world around us, particularly in aerospace and transport, but also in architecture.

Slime mould spores. Coloured SEM of spores
(orange) of the slime mould *Badhamia utricularis*.
The spores are associated with a mass of threads
(the thin white strands), which in this species contain
calcium oxide. Changes in the moisture content
of the air cause the threads to change shape, flicking
spores into the air and helping them to disperse.
Slime moulds are not fungi, but a separate group
with complex life cycles.

Coloured SEM of human blood showing red and white cells, and platelets. The red blood cells have a characteristic disc shape that is concave on both sides, and they are numerous. These large cells contain haemoglobin, a red pigment by which oxygen is transported around the body.

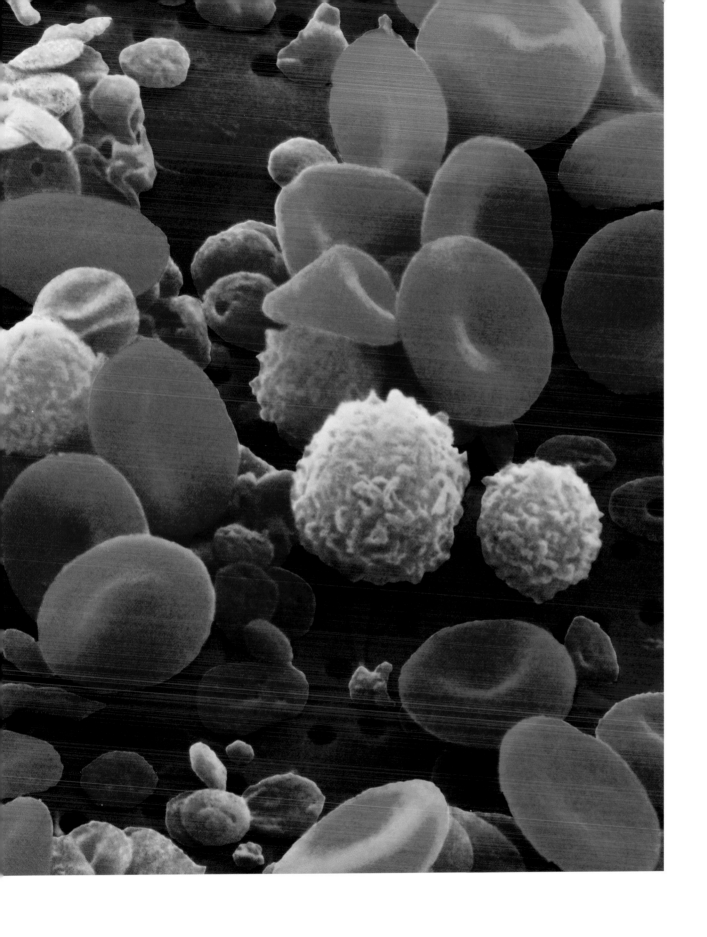

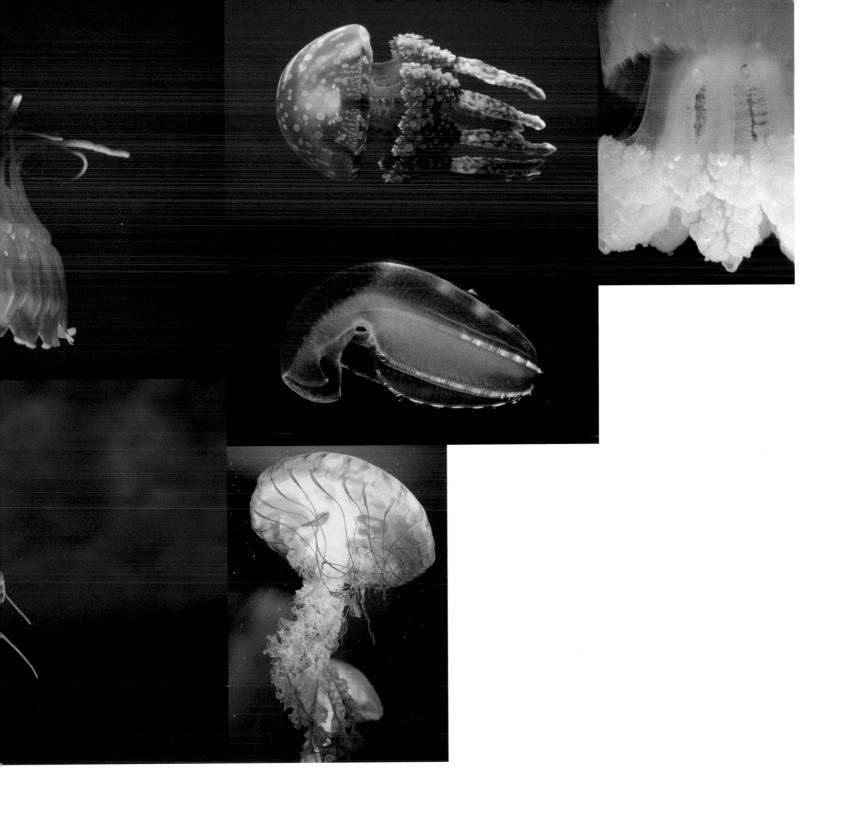

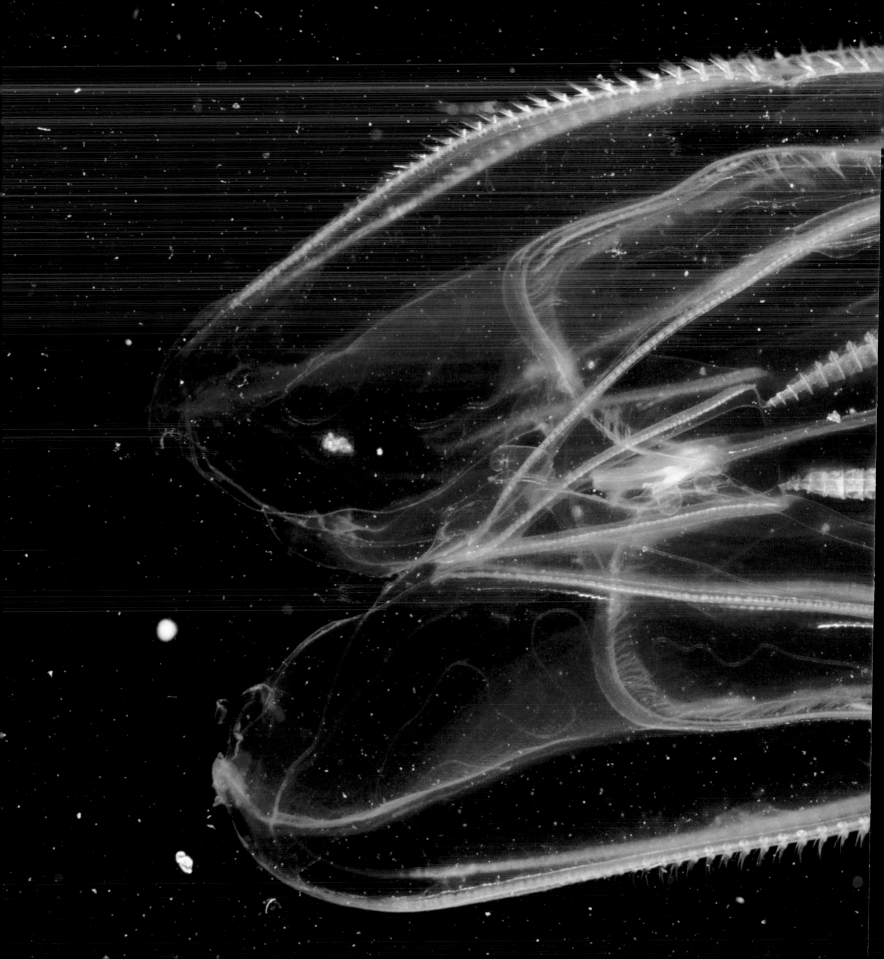

The sea walnut (*Mnemiopsis leidyi*) is a species belonging to the ctenophores – it is not a jellyfish, although it resembles one. Sea walnuts contain special cells, or photocytes, that produce bioluminescence. During the day this light shines in various colours along eight comb-like bands on their bodies. At night, they glide through the water like oscillating lanterns, emitting phosphorescent green or blue light.

A chandelier made from diamonds (above) – and a close-up of the
Eden project structure in the UK (right). References to the natural
world abound in contemporary design and architecture.

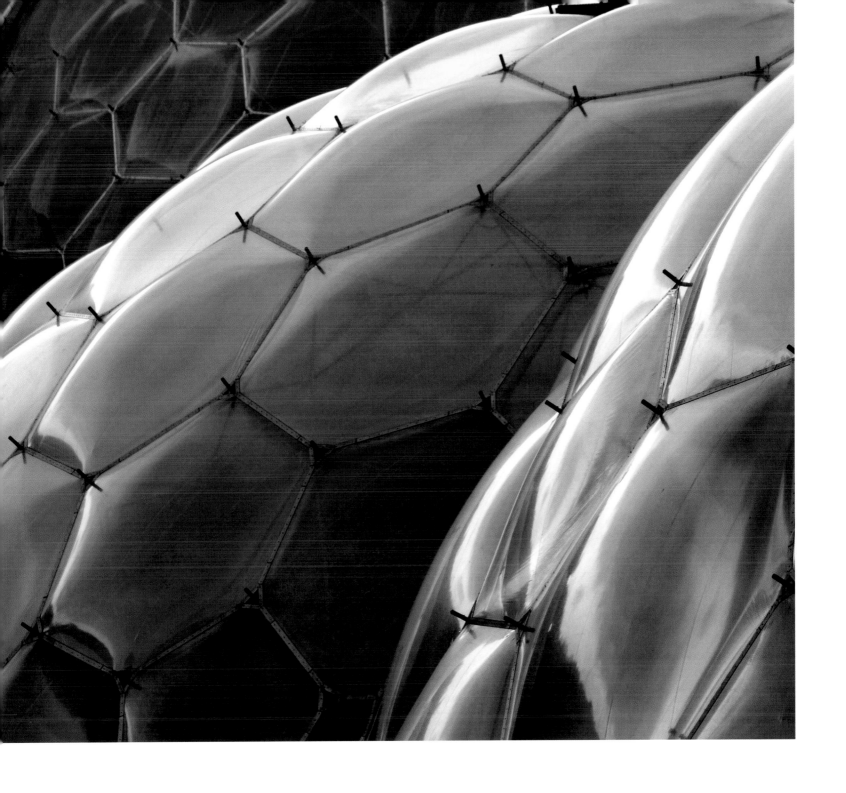

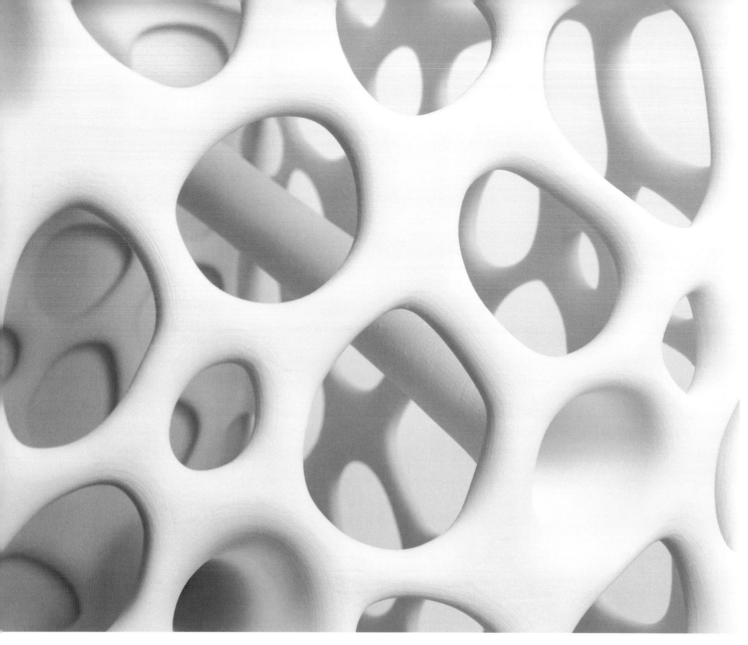

Above and right — Manufacturing methods are starting to allow designers to 'grow' structure and shape in similar fashion to naturally occurring forms.

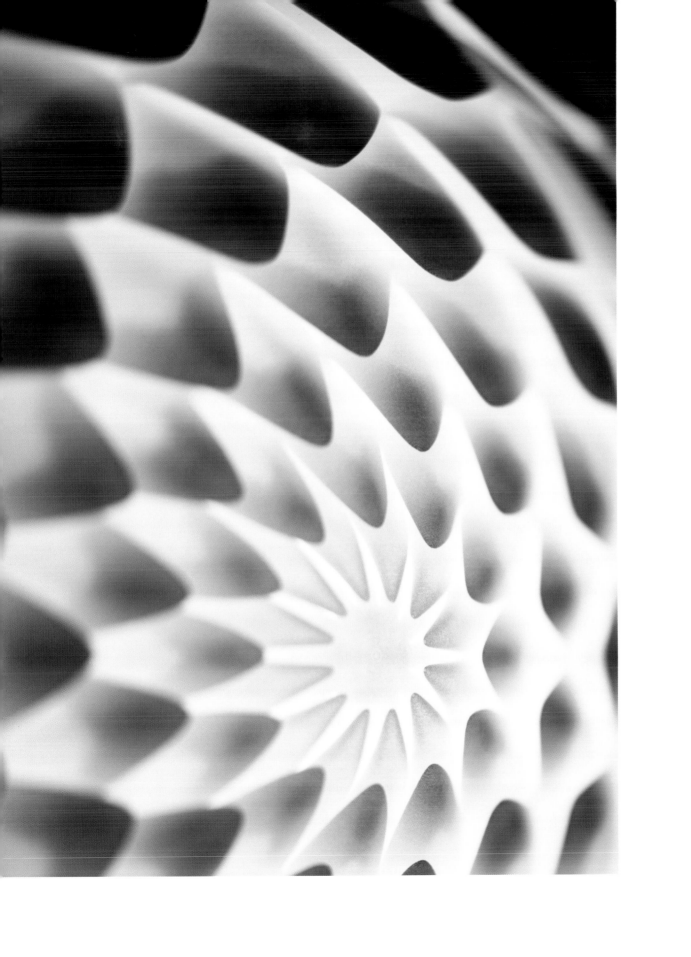

Good morning
Good evening
Good afternoon
the time in
London is
New York is
Tokyo is
twenty
zero
nine
two
twelve
eight
six
eleven
three
seven
fif
thir
teen
ten
one
hours
and
fifty
eleven
twenty
forty
three
five
twelve
six
nine
seven
one
four
thir
fif
teen
Tick
zero
two
minutes
Tock

The British product designer Sam Buxton's SIOS (Surface
Intelligent Objects) work uses photoluminescence to create active
surfaces on familiar objects, blurring the boundaries between
display screens and the physical environment. Shown here are his
'Word Clock' and 'Electroluminescent Table'. The clock celebrates
the passage of time, while the table not only displays information
but also reacts to objects placed on it.

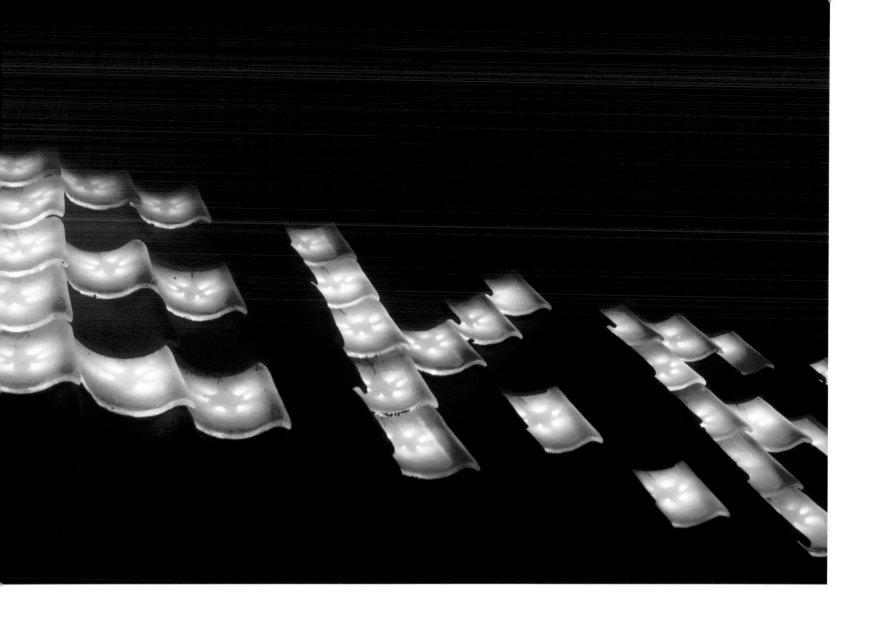

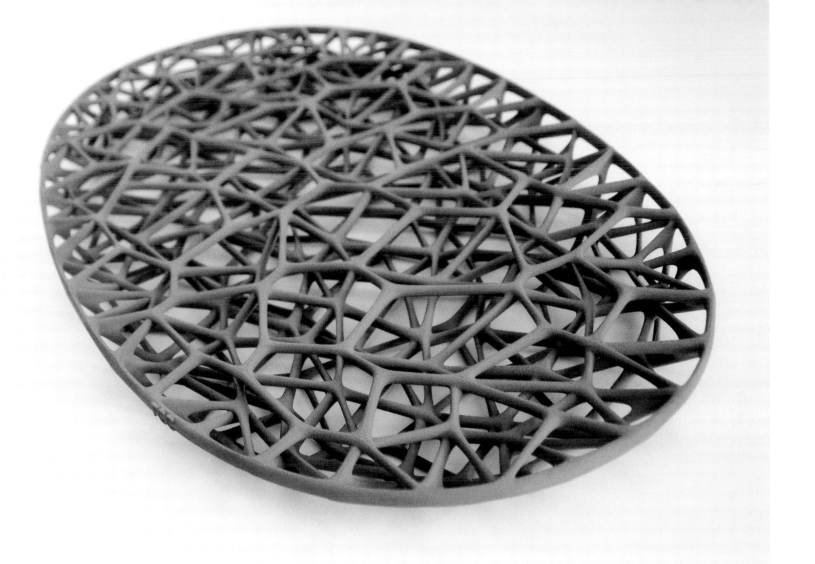

Left — Rapid prototyped sculpture.

Right — Close-up from the natural world.

The ethereal shapes found through microphotography are echoed in shapes produced through rapid prototyping. A new industrial revolution is rapidly evolving in which the designer, through the miracle of the digital world, is liberated from the traditional constraints of high volumes and high tooling costs.

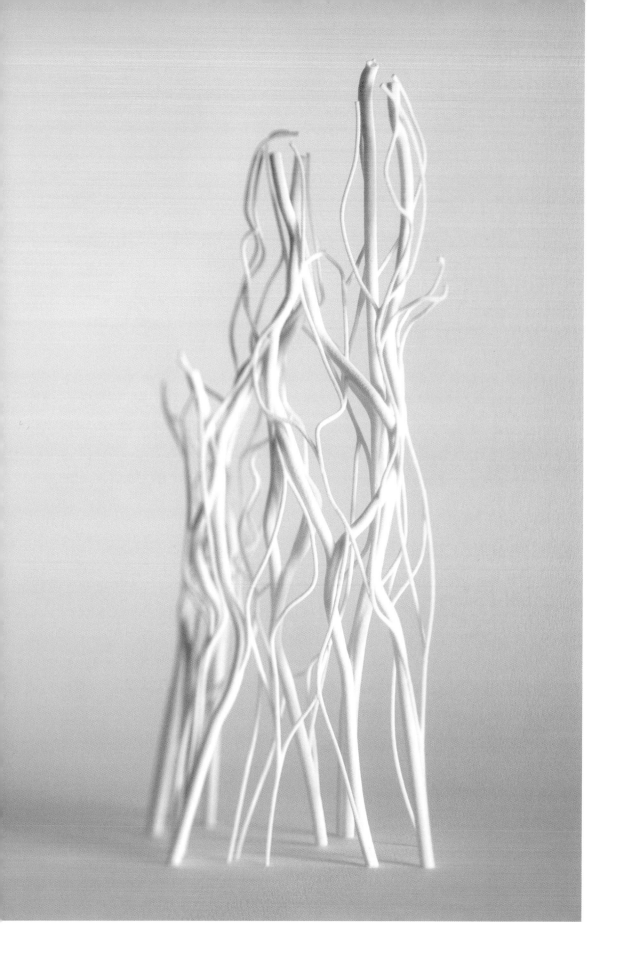

New frontiers —

The subject of the moment, in terms of the future of design, is rapid prototyping. This is a catch-all description for a series of complex technologies that allow the manufacture of an object directly from a computer file. Using lasers to solidify liquid or powdered polymers in layers has made it suddenly possible to create objects that until now, though possible to imagine, would have been difficult if not impossible to make using conventional manufacturing processes.

The more forward-looking designers and manufacturers envision an extraordinary new dawn, where products and ideas are materialized at will, customized to their user's specification or altered to suit the individual. Pessimistic future-watchers, on the other hand, predict even more oceans of useless stuff for people to consume thoughtlessly.

Whichever way it goes, the current hyperactivity in this field makes for a fascinating leap forward in potential for designers, no more so than in the experiments by the Belgium-based company Freedom of Creation. It has been encouraging artists, designers and even mathematicians to push the boundaries of the three-dimensional object using the latest selective laser sintering (SLS) techniques. Here we see the new frontier of manufacturing – not just rapid prototyping, but rapid manufacturing. The ultimate goal is no longer to make or sell a fixed object, but to be able to sell an electronic file containing a set of parameters. These will define an object that can be adapted by the buyer and manufactured locally in the nearest rapid-manufacturing facility.

The crazy Swedish collective Front pushes the boundaries in proposing a tool by which a piece of furniture is drawn physically in three dimensions by holding a marker and describing a chair or coat hanger in space. The marker is read by a scanner which translates the gesture into code, thus producing a file that allows for the rapid manufacturing of the product, which, as with the fairy godmother and her magic wand, appears out of thin air. And – kerpow! – the furniture business is suddenly transformed. Not only is the whole process of design shifted into the realm of theatre and mime, but also the industrial manufacturing process is able to produce each piece as a complete original, rather than as part of a batch or manufacturing lot. Anybody and everybody are liberated to create and make.

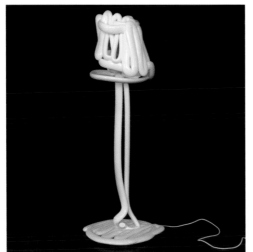

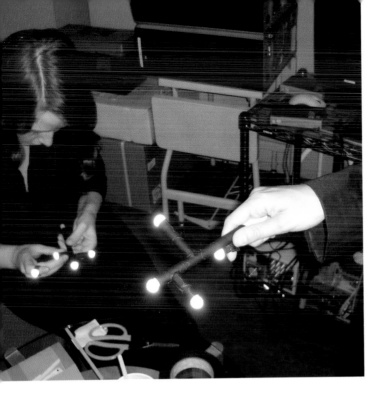

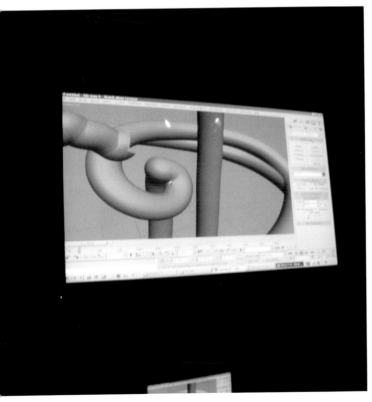
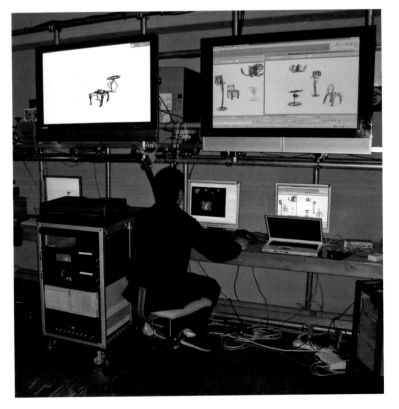

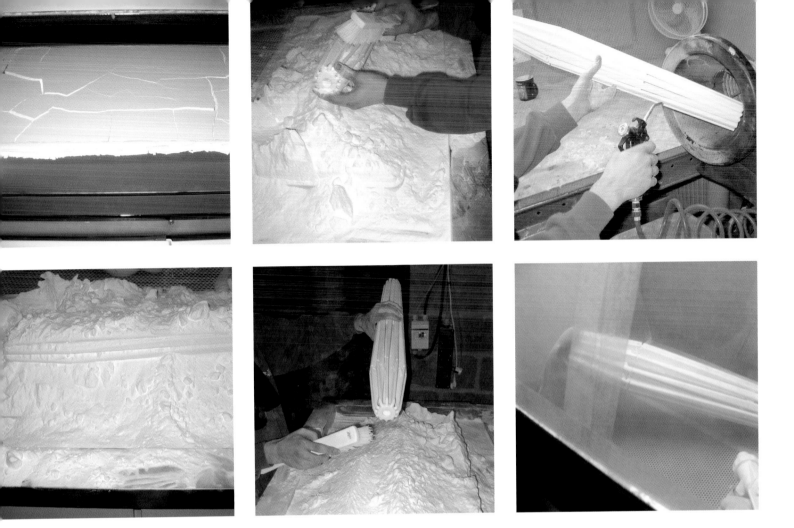

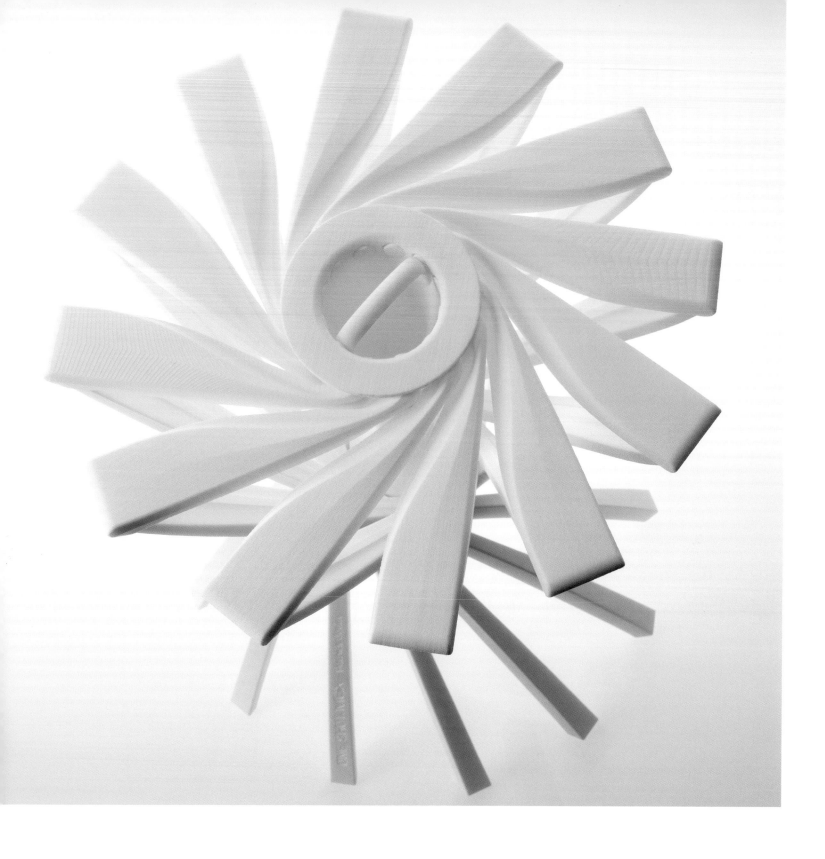

The publisher would like to thank the following contributors for their kind permission to reproduce the photographs in this book.

Page 3 above Jacob Dahlgren
3 below left John Pratt/Keystone Features/Getty Images
3 below right Albrecht Durer/Private Collection, Lauros/Giraudon/ The Bridgeman Art Library, London
11 Mary Evans Picture Library
12 Ricardo Beliel/Brazil Photos/Alamy
13–15 Tom Dixon
16–18 Bryan & Cherry Alexander Photography/Alamy
19 Tom Dixon
20 Marc Hill/Alamy
21 Joshua Kucera
22 Krishnendu Halder/Reuters/Corbis
23 Jim Zuckerman/Alamy
24 Tom Dixon
25 Michael Yamashita/Corbis
26 David Williams/Alamy
27 Horizon International Images Ltd/Alamy
28–29 Robert Harding Picture Library/Alamy
30 Tom Dixon
31 mediacolor's/Alamy
32 a + b Tom Dixon
32 c Tom Dixon (Artist: Joanne Tinker)
32 d Neal Wilson/Construction Photography
32 e Robert Brook/Alamy
33–45 Tom Dixon
46 Charles O'Rear/Corbis
47 Tom Dixon
48 ICP/Alamy
49–50 Tom Dixon
51 Felicia Shelton (feliciaworldwide@mac.com)
52 Tom Dixon (Des: Thomas Heatherwick)
53 ITP Images/Construction Photography
54 Raj Patidar/Reuters/Corbis
55–59 Tom Dixon
60 Carmen de la Ca/Alamy
61 blickwinkel/Alamy
62–63 Tom Dixon
64 blickwinkel/Alamy
65 David Fleetham/Alamy
66 imagebroker/Alamy
67 Suzanne Long/Alamy
68 tbkmedia.de/Alamy
69 Raoul Kramer (Des: Studio Libertiny)
70–71 Tom Dixon
72 a Tom Dixon
72 b Freedom of Creation
72 c–e Tom Dixon
73 a Tom Dixon
73 b Ron Arad & Associates Ltd.
73 c + d Tom Dixon
74 Tom Dixon
75 blickwinkel/Alamy
76–78 Tom Dixon
79 Freedom of Creation
80 Studio Tord Boontje
81 London Glass Blowing (Des: Peter Layton)
82–85 Tom Dixon
86 Thomas Duval (Des: Patrick Jouin)
87 Keg Karleung Wai (07742260345/Karleung.wai@gmail.com)
88 Freedom of Creation

89 Ton Kinsbergen/Science Photo Library
90–92 Tom Dixon
93 Tom Dixon (Des: Thomas Heatherwick)
94 Swarovski
95–101 Tom Dixon
103–105 Nils Jorgensen/Rex Features
106–107 ©Courtesy of Anish Kapoor Studio
108 ph: Jan Uvelius, Malmo, Sweden. ©Courtesy of Antony Gormley & Jay Jopling/White Cube, London & Galleri Andersson Sandstrom Umedalen Sculpture Foundation, Umea, Sweden
109 ph: Steve White, London ©Courtesy of Antony Gormley & Jay Jopling/ White Cube, London
110–113 ©Courtesy of David Mach
121 Tom Dixon
122 Dr Mark J Winter/Science Photo Library
123 David Taylor/Science Photo Library
124 Science Museum Library
125 Science Photo Library
126 Science Museum Library
127–129 Richard Sweeney
131 Interfoto Pressebildagentur/Alamy
132 a Juniors Bildarchiv/Alamy
132 b Greg Philpott/Alamy
132 c SC Photos/Alamy
132 d Holt Studios International Ltd/Alamy
133 above Jake Norton/Alamy
133 below Chris Gomersall/Alamy
134 mediacolor's/Alamy
135 David R Frazier Photolibrary Inc/Alamy
136–137 ©Courtesy of Antony Gormley & Jay Jopling/White Cube, London & Caldic Collectie, Rotterdam, Holland
138 Felicia Shelton
139 Kenneth Cobonpue
140 Jacques Jangoux/Alamy
141 Patrick Ward/Alamy
142 Tom Dixon
143 ITP Images/Construction Photography
144–145 China Photos/Getty Images
146 Lou Linwei/Alamy
147 China Images/Alamy
148 Takanori Sekine/AFP/Getty Images
149 Greg Baker/AFP/Getty Images
150 Keystone/Getty Images
151–153 Tom Dixon
154 Truck/Rogers Marvel Architects
155 Vario Images GmbH & Co/Alamy
156–157 Tom Dixon
158 Felicia Shelton
159 Tom Dixon
160–161 I-Beam Design
163–165 Courtesy of Thomas Goreau www.globalcoral.org
166 Tom Dixon
167 Taken from 'Woodwork in Theory & Practice' by John A Walton. Harrap & Co Ltd 1963. Stanley Works, New York
168 Tom Dixon
169 left Emil Pozar/Alamy
169 above right Tom Dixon
169 below right Peter Steiner/Alamy
170 A A World Travel Library/Alamy
171 Bygonetimes/Alamy
172–173 Percy Ryall/Alamy
174 Ray Roberts/Alamy
175 Tom Powel Imaging (Artist: John Powers)

Page 497 f Tom Dixon
497 g Jamie Kripke/Corbis
497 h Nicola Dove/Millennium Images
498 left Janine Wiedel Photolibrary/Alamy
498 above right Tom Dixon
498 below right + 499 above ©Niki Medlik, Taken from Trevor Naylor, Living
Normally: Where Life Comes Before Style, Thames & Hudson Ltd, London
499 below Tom Dixon
500–503 Felicia Shelton
504 Tom Dixon
505 Felicia Shelton
507 Susumu Koshimizu (Arch: Akemi Katsuno & Takashi Yagi,
Love the Life)
508 Mikael Karlsson/Alamy
509 Andrew Milligan/PA Archive/PA Photos
510–511 Mikael Karlsson/Alamy
512 Chad Ehlers/Alamy
513 Barry Lewis/Alamy
514–515 David Alan Harvey/Magnum Photos
516–517 Guy Stubbs/Indpendent Contributors/africanpictures.net
518 Sperc
519 Sydney Seshibedi/AfriLife/africanpictures.net
520–523 Hanse Haus GmbH
524 Tasuo Iwaoka
525–527 Dietmar Tollerian (Arch: Andreas Strauss)
528–529 Sascha Kletzsch ©Richard Horden. All rights reserved.
Arch: Horden Cherry Lee, London/Haack+Hopfner, Munich.
www.microcompacthome.com
530 Trip/Alamy
532–536 Urban Space Management
537 Roland Tannier/Freitag
538–539 Urban Space Management
540 Kisho Kurokawa Architect & Associates
541–547 Tomio Ohashi (Kisho Kurokawa Architect & Associates)
548 Kisho Kurokawa Architect & Associates
549 easyGroup IP Licensing Ltd
550–551 Inflate
552–553 Tom Dixon
554–557 Rainer Mader/Archenova
559–561 ©Courtesy of Martin Creed
562 ©Courtesy of Michael Landy & Thomas Dane Gallery, London
563 above ph: Vron Harris ©Michael Landy 2001.
Commissioned & produced by Artangel
563 below ©Courtesy of Michael Landy & Thomas Dane Gallery, London
564–565 Ransmeier & Floyd
566 Felicia Shelton
567 Marcel Sigel (www.marcelsigel.com/www.zuii.com)
568 Robots, Italy
569 Michael Marriott
570–571 Kyouei Design (Des: Kouichi Okamoto)
572 Marcel Sigel (www.marcelsigel.com/www.zuii.com)
573–574 Arik Levy
575 Joe Nunn (www.tobeofuse.org)
576–577 Ken Kirkwood/Vitsoe
578–579 Oxfam
580 Russell Gordon/Danita Delimont/Alamy
581–582 Blaine Harrington III/Alamy
583 Keren Su/China Span/Alamy
584 Graeme Williams/South Photographs/africanpictures.net
585 Joerg Reuther/Imagebroker/Alamy
586 Urban Space Management
587 Philip Pegden/Alamy
594 V&A Images, Victoria & Albert Museum, London

595 JA Hampton/Hulton Archive/Getty Images
596 Evans/Three Lions/Getty Images
597 Kim Kulish/AP/PA Photos
598 Sony/Getty Images
599 Popperfoto/Getty Images
600 Peter King/Getty Images
601 Popperfoto/Getty Images
602 Keystone/Getty Images
603 Alfred Eisenstaedt/Pix Inc/Time & Life/Getty Images
604 Estate of Buckminster Fuller
605 Used with permission of The Frank R Paul Estate
606 Mary Evans Picture Library
607–611 NASA
612–617 NASA AMES Research Centre
618 Tom Vack/Colani Trading AG
619–620 Colani Trading AG
621 MetroNaps UK
622 Kadu Niemeyer/Arcaid (Arch: Oscar Niemeyer)
624–625 Jorge Ferrari/epa/Corbis
626–627 Barrie Rokeach/Alamy
628–629 Tom Dixon
630–631 Lambert Kamps
632–635 Tom Dixon
636 Courtesy of Silken Hotels (Arch: Zaha Hadid)
637 Peter Bennetts (Paul Morgan Architects)
638 Morphosis
639 Ben Foster/Eden Project
640 Lou Linwei/Alamy
641 Tom Dixon
642 Steve Gschmeissner/Science Photo Library
643–645 Eye of Science/Science Photo Library
646 Steve Gschmeissner/Science Photo Library
647 Eye of Science/Science Photo Library
649 National Cancer Institute/Science Photo Library
650 left Chris Martin-Bahr/Science Photo Library
650 above + below right Bill Curtsinger/National Geographic Stock
651 a David Doubilet/National Geographic Stock
651 b Tim Laman/National Geographic Stock
651 c Bill Curtsinger/National Geographic Stock
651 d Gilbert S Grant/Science Photo Library
652–653 George Grall/National Geographic Stock
654 Swarovski
655 Marc Hill/Alamy
656–657 Freedom of Creation
658–659 Swarovski
660–661 Sam Buxton
662–663 Lambert Kamps
664–665 Freedom of Creation
666 Materialise, MGX(Des: R&Sie)
667 Eye of Science/Science Photo Library
668–669 Materialise, MGX(Des: R&Sie)
670 Eddie Ryle-Hodges/Leslie Garland Picture Library/Alamy
671 Tom Dixon
673–675 Front
676–677 Materialise, MGX
678 a–f Materialise, MGX
678 g–i + 679 + 680 Thomas Duval (Des: Patrick Jouin)

Every effort has been made to trace the copyright holders. We apologize
in advance for any unintentional omissions and would be pleased to insert
the appropriate acknowledgement in any subsequent publication.

Publisher: Lorraine Dickey
Tom Dixon's Consultant: Pippa Toolan
Managing Editor: Sybella Marlow
Copy Editor: Alison Wormleighton
Art Director: Jonathan Christie
Design: Graphic Thought Facility, London
Illustration: Mia Nilsson
Inside cover photography: Patrice Hanicotte
Picture Research: Demelza Hill, Anne-Marie Hoines
Production Manager: Katherine Hockley

Printed in China